Corrective Reading

Enrichment SRA Blackline Masters

Decoding B1 Decoding Strategies

Siegfried Engelmann

Gary Johnson

McGraw Hill SRA

Columbus, OH

SRAonline.com

Printed in the United States of America.

Send all inquiries to this address:
SRA/McGraw-Hill
4400 Easton Commons
Columbus, OH 43219

ISBN: 978-0-07-611223-4
MHID: 0-07-611223-3

4 5 6 7 8 9 MAL 13 12 11 10 09

The *McGraw·Hill* Companies

Contents

Contents

Corrective Reading
Decoding B1
Enrichment Blackline Masters

Note to the Teacher

The activities in this book reinforce the skills taught in the 2008 edition of the Corrective Reading Decoding B1 program. Each activity provides practice in an essential reading skill, such as

- recognition of sounds and sound combinations
- word identification
- correct spelling of words
- spelling of words with endings, such as **s, ed, ing, er, ly,** and **en**
- spelling of root words without those endings
- writing compound and other two-part words
- writing sentences
- answering comprehension questions about story passages
- demonstrating comprehension of details in stories
- sequencing activities in a story
- identifying main characters
- building oral reading fluency

(Skills are identified at the bottom of each page.)

The materials are designed to be completed as study-time homework assignments. The students are not to use the Student Book when completing the Blackline Master. (The *Decoding B1* Student Book and Workbook should usually remain at school.) The Blackline Master pages correspond by lesson number to the *Decoding B1* lesson numbers. The Blackline Masters should be assigned as homework on the same day that the corresponding lesson is completed at school.

Students should be able to complete the homework assignments without any special instructions from the teacher or from a parent. In Lessons 1, 2, 4, and 20, a note to the parent at the bottom of the page directs the parent to ask the student what sound should be circled in the first row of letters and what word should be circled in the second row. All other exercises can be completed without additional instructions.

Timed Reading

To provide additional practice in building oral reading fluency, someone at home can listen to the student read aloud. These timed readings begin at Lesson 16. The procedure is similar to that of the regular program timed readings, which begin at Lesson 16. The passage that appears in the second page of the Blackline Master for Lessons 16 through 65 is taken from the first part of the story from the previous lesson. For Lesson 16, students read part of the story from Lesson 15 at home, and so forth. The student reads aloud for one minute to a parent or listener who follows along and signals when the student is to stop. The number of words read in one minute and the number of errors are recorded, and the parent/listener signs at the bottom of the page. The student brings the signed page to school on the next school day as part of the daily two-page homework assignment.

Checking Homework

The homework should be checked each day. The most efficient procedure is to conduct a teacher-directed group workcheck. Use the annotated answer key beginning on page 117 of this book. Monitor students as they mark their own papers. Scan students' written responses for accuracy and legibility.

- For exercises that require the writing of whole words or word parts, call on individual students to spell the words as they should appear in the answers.
- For comprehension items, call on individual students to read each question and say the correct answer.
- For activities in which students fill in the missing words in a passage, call on individual students to read the passage aloud and say the word that should appear in the blank.

If the group is large, read the correct answers for each item as students check their own papers.

Homework Chart and Point System

Keep a record of the completed homework assignments. A reproducible Homework Chart appears on page viii. Or you may elect to have students record points in the Point Chart in their Workbooks. Points earned can be recorded in the bonus box for the regular lesson.

Points could be awarded as follows:

completing homework	2 points
0 errors	2 points
1 or 2 errors	1 point
more than 2 errors	0 points

When the timed readings begin at Lesson 16:

completing the homework reading checkout	2 points

If you award points for homework assignments, you will need to modify the number of points required in the regular program to earn various letter grades. (For a discussion of the points and letter grades, see the discussion under "The Management System" in the Decoding B1 Teacher's Guide.) An alternative procedure would be to make the points earned for homework assignments separate from those earned in the regular program and to provide special incentives for completing homework.

The Blackline Master homework pages are designed so that students can be successful. Once students learn that they can complete homework successfully, they will be motivated to continue to do so. If the teacher provides positive verbal feedback for completing homework assignments, along with the use of points, students will be encouraged to do well, and their reading performance will continue to improve.

Letter to Parents

A letter explaining the general procedures for homework assignments appears on the following page. This letter should be sent home along with the first homework assignment.

Dear Parents,

Students are expected to complete homework as part of their reading lessons. The homework activities provide practice in important reading skills. In the daily homework exercises, students receive practice in the following reading skills:

- identifying the sounds of single letters and the sounds of letter combinations
- identifying words
- spelling words with endings and words without endings
- writing sentences
- answering questions about story passages
- building oral reading fluency

For Lessons 1 through 15, students complete one page of homework exercises for each lesson. Starting at Lesson 16, the homework consists of two pages. On the second page is a story passage that the student is to read aloud to someone at home. This activity provides practice on speed and accuracy.

You will need a digital watch, a digital timer (such as a kitchen timer), or a clock with a sweep second hand so that you can time the student for exactly 1 minute. The student starts at the first word of the passage and reads for 1 minute. You count the mistakes the student makes. The goal is for the student to read exactly what is on the page.

Here are the kinds of errors to count:

- saying the wrong word or mispronouncing a word
- adding a word
- leaving out a word
- adding an ending to a word (for example, reading "plays" for play)
- leaving off an ending (for example, reading "start" for started)
- not stopping at the end of a sentence
- rereading part of a sentence

At the end of 1 minute, stop the student. Write the number of words read in 1 minute and the number of errors in the blanks at the bottom of the page.

If the student wants to read the passage again, write the number of times the passage was read in the blank at the bottom of the page.

Sign at the bottom of the page. The student should return the homework assignment to school on the next school day.

Remember to be patient. Students who try hard need to know that they are improving. Your assistance each day will help the student improve. The more practice the student receives, the faster the student will become a better reader.

Thank you.

Corrective Reading   Decoding B1 Homework Chart

Teacher _____   Group _____

Student	Date	Lesson Number																											

Name _____

Part 1

Match the words.

seeds •   • last

last •   • man

man •   • lip

cat •   • seeds

lip •   • cat

Part 2

(s) o e s t p l m n a a w e r s p k u b s w q a z d r t y u n b g t y u p l n a z d s e s (5)

(clap) t a o q a s c l a p m f f r t y u p l l a c l a p q e r t s v b l a t c l a p d o x e c l a p s (4)

Part 3

Copy the sentences.

Keep a plant in that sack.

_____

Can the cat sleep in a lap?

_____

Fill this pan with sticks.

_____

Directions, part 2: Ask the student, "What sound will you circle in the first row?" (sss) "What word will you circle in the second row?" (clap)

Part 1
Match the words.

lamp   •   •   sleep

feeds   •   •   stick

sleep   •   •   clap

stick   •   •   lamp

clap   •   •   feeds

Part 2

(i) eljaioatrfisdeircbpliteaghhnmaliomnbgreijlide (7)

(sit) selfitsithatsitinfitsisittisetsifefigmissatisitif (4)

(this) hitthehiminthisitisteethifthisthatpitdidthisinis (3)

Part 3
Copy the sentences.

Dad can see the cats sleep.

_____

Plant this seed in the sand.

_____

Did that tack stick the cat?

_____

This ant sits in a back pack.

_____

Directions, part 2: Ask the student, "What sound will you circle in the first row?" (ĭĭĭ) "What word will you circle in the second row?" (sit) "What word will you circle in the third row?" (this)

Name _____

Part 1
Copy the sentences.

This cap fits in that pack.

_____

We had no plan for a trip.

_____

That truck can go so fast.

_____

Part 2
Read the sentences in the box.   **Write the first word of these sentences.**

1. At last she has a black cat.
2. Will that truck slip in mud?
3. Slip this stick in the pack.

2nd sentence _____

1st sentence _____

3rd sentence _____

Part 3
Match the words.

math ●   ● cash

hill ●   ● teeth

cash ●   ● math

truck ●   ● hill

teeth ●   ● truck

Writing sentences, writing words, matching words

Name _____

Part 1

(sh)   d e f a c l p o e s h s e a s h m n j s a s h e i p l t h n z s l s h f d s h f e c r q w   (5)

(flag) d w f l a g e r o p l e g c z d a f l a g j h e r c l a m c l p e f l a g s a t e f l a t v b s p   (3)

Part 2

Copy the sentences.

Will that milk last us for a week?

_____

I need a pack for the trip.

_____

Three deer sleep with the sheep.

_____

Part 3

Match the words and complete them.

truck   ●   ●   sh

sheep   ●   ●   mi

milk   ●   ●   ant

drink   ●   ●   ink

plant   ●   ●   tru

Directions, part 1: Ask the student, "What sound will you circle in the first row?" (sh) "What word will you circle in the second row?" (flag)

4   *Lesson 4*

Name _____

Part 1
Match the words and complete them.

stop   ●————————————●   ink

flag   ●————————————●   ore

drink   ●————————————●   fl

truck   ●————————————●   st

store   ●————————————●   uck

Part 2
Copy the sentences.

We will go for more fish at the store.

_____

She sat with me at the track meet.

_____

Is he free to go with us?

_____

Part 3
Read the sentences in the box.

Write the first word of these sentences.

1. I will fill this gas can.
2. Can we go to the store?
3. She had a fun trip.

3rd sentence _____

1st sentence _____

2nd sentence _____

Writing words, copying sentences

Name _____

Part 1

Copy the sentences.

The junk did not fit in that truck.

_____

Will Pat feed the cats?

_____

A steep hill had grass on it.

_____

His feet feel sore and cold.

_____

Part 2

(on) l i n r s t a n b c s o n a t h e h l u l o n e t a c k o n a e l i n o l s d o n r a o n a o n l e (6)

(for) o n f o r t s f o r l d t o t e f o r o r t a l f o r k f a n e f o r l p k d o f o r t a s f i (6)

(to) s o t o d p f o s a w t o k e t a o w a l t h t o s h t o u s h t r c t o j p i a t o e h t o a (7)

Part 3

Read the sentences in the box.

1. The man told him, "Hop in this truck."
2. Pat said, "He will feed the cat."
3. She said, "Fill this sack with fish."

Write the first word of these sentences.

2nd sentence _____

1st sentence _____

3rd sentence _____

Writing sentences, finding words, writing words

Name _____

Part 1
Match the words and complete them.

_____ sing ●	● clo _____
_____ hill ●	● ch _____
_____ cheer ●	● sa _____
_____ clock ●	● ng _____
_____ sack ●	● ll _____

Part 2
Read the sentences in the box.

1. Fold that green rag.
2. How much cash do you have?
3. That man has an old cat.

Write the first word of these sentences.

1st sentence _____

3rd sentence _____

2nd sentence _____

Part 3
Copy the sentences.

How did she do in the math class?

_____

That man has more cats than I have.

_____

Fill this sack with fish.

_____

Will she sell that horse this week?

_____

Writing words, copying sentences

(ch) oischndsndrchshadthchesaichwhcritheichopshtch (6)

(th) utotheonisnidchthheptoshttoethshetohestholthr (5)

(ing) kmsdaitoingratishingtmattomeingscinpisxdinger (4)

Part 2
Copy the sentences.

She is sending me to the meeting at the shop.

_____

We do not have the list with us.

_____

His truck has a bad dent in the top.

_____

She ran fast at the track meet.

_____

Part 3
Match the words and complete them.

when	●	●	ch
chip	●	●	ift
crab	●	●	wh
fold	●	●	ab
lift	●	●	old

Finding letters, writing sentences, matching words

Name _____

Part 1

Read the sentences in the box.

1. When will we win a track meet?
2. They were not singing.
3. Can you sell that truck?

Write the first word of these sentences.

2nd sentence _____

3rd sentence _____

1st sentence _____

Part 2

Copy the sentences.

The bus went faster than the old truck.

_____

Which letter did you send her?

_____

Bring them back to class in the morning.

_____

That man was the last person on the bus.

_____

Part 3

Match the words and complete them.

_____ shop	●	●	mu
_____ ranch	●	●	op
_____ much	●	●	eet
_____ lift	●	●	ch
_____ sheet	●	●	li

Writing words, writing sentences, matching words

Name _____

Part 1

Copy the sentences.

Were you in the street after the truck crash?

_____

The cat will drink the milk in that pan.

_____

What did that woman tell you to do?

_____

After a nap, he felt much better.

_____

Part 2

Read the sentences in the box.

| 1. Was she with him when you met her? |
| 2. They sell chips in that store. |
| 3. Bring me that glass of milk. |

Write the first word of these sentences.

1st sentence _____

3rd sentence _____

2nd sentence _____

Part 3

(was) h e w a s d i p s a w w a s i t w e s a w l e t w a s h o r s e w a s a t m e t ④

(you) w e y e s i f y o u w h a t t h e y t o f o r y o u o f w h a t y o w a y o u ③

(er) a f t e r d r e s s c a t s e r o s e l l e r s h e l l s e t b t e r c l e r h e s ⑤

(this) a t t a p t h i s d a d t h i f t h i s p a n a m t h i s s h e t h e t h i s h ④

Writing sentences, writing words, finding words

Part 1

Match the words and complete them.

rancher   ●————————●   th

going   ●————————●   elf

path   ●————————●   ranch

shelf   ●————————●   go

Part 2

Copy the sentences.

The horse jumped over the creek.

_____

Tim fell into the creek when the horse jumped.

_____

Part 3

(of)   o n f o r t h i s t o p o f a f t e r p o n d y o y h r s e c o t o f t o l d o n o f y   ③

(said)   s a n d s i d s a i d h a d s a d s a i d s l i p s i s a t s a i d s l o w s t o p s a i d   ④

(how)   h o p h o t n o w h o w s h o p f l o w h o p h o w s h o t o w h s l o w c r o w   ②

Part 4

Read the sentences in the box.   **Write the last word of these sentences.**

1. Just then, his sister yelled.
2. Where is the red broom?
3. He told her what to do.

2nd sentence _____

3rd sentence _____

1st sentence _____

Writing words, copying sentences, finding words, writing words

Name _____

Part 1

Read the sentences in the box.

> 1. Tim went to the trash can.
> 2. His sister gave orders.
> 3. He began to sweep.

Write the last word of these sentences.

3rd sentence _____

1st sentence _____ **can** _____

2nd sentence _____

Part 2

Copy the sentences.

Tim got the broom and began to sweep.

_____

He told his sister what to do.

_____

His sister got mad and yelled at him.

_____

Part 3

(do) t h e t o i t d i m d o w a s d o d i d s e e d a d d o t o l d s i t d o c l i p i d o ⑤

(one) c o r n o f t o d e e r o n e o r o n h i s o n e t o t o r n i t o n e s a o n e n o ④

Part 4

Match the words and complete them.

where ●   ● tra

master ●   ● order

trash ●   ● mast

orders ●   ● ere

Writing words, copying sentences, finding words

Name _____

Part 1

Copy the sentences.

What do you think is in this trash can?

_____

She filled a sack with shells.

_____

His mom told him what happened.

_____

Part 2

Read the sentences in the box.

1. These socks go with black slacks.
2. He had red socks for running.
3. His little sister grinned.
4. Ron's mom was not glad.

Write the last word of these sentences.

2nd sentence _____

4th sentence _____

3rd sentence _____

1st sentence _____

Part 3

Match the words and complete them.

_____ there   •   •   per

_____ asked   •   •   fore

_____ before   •   •   ked

_____ person   •   •   ere

Copying sentences, writing words, matching words

Name _____

Part 1

Read the sentences in the box.

1. Get that ice out of my pocket.
2. At last, she stopped.
3. Now I will help you.
4. How did she do that?

Write the last word of these sentences.

4th sentence _____

2nd sentence _____

1st sentence _____

3rd sentence _____

Part 2

Match the words and complete them.

_____ still ●	● pt _____
_____ kept ●	● ill _____
_____ drop ●	● ll _____
_____ well ●	● dr _____

Part 3

Copy the sentences.

He had a big chunk of ice in his bag.

_____

She helped the rat hop.

_____

How do you think she did that?

_____

Writing words, matching words, copying sentences

Name _____

Part 1

(ed) a f t e r e d t u s h e d r l h e r l o e d p n m c v e d w r e r a e d t o u e d b c i e s (6)

(lie) c h l i d s l i e d i d n o g u m l i e n o t h e l i e s a t l i p l i e l i f t l i e s (5)

(are) h o w t h e n a n t a r e a n d a r e r e d c a b a t r a m s a r e r a t s a r e a n (4)

Part 2

The words in the first column have endings.
Write the same words without endings in the second column.

shipped

slipper

hopping

clapped

Part 3

Read the sentences in the box.

1. Sandy went to the store.
2. The rat ate at a fast rate.
3. She gave the rat oats.
4. The rat chomped and chomped.

Write the last word of these sentences.

4th sentence _____

1st sentence _____

3rd sentence _____

2nd sentence _____

Part 4

Copy the sentence.

She gave the rat oats with gum on them.

_____

Finding words, suffixes, writing words, copying sentences

Name _____

Part 1

Read the sentences in the box.

1. She got a rat that ate.
2. That rat ate at a fast rate.
3. Sandy dropped the rat into a box.
4. The rat bit Sandy on the nose.

Write the last word of these sentences.

4th sentence _____

1st sentence _____

3rd sentence _____

2nd sentence _____

Part 2

(ea)   s e e m t o e a h e a r h e a l r a t e h e r e a r s e r a e s t o w e a t c f e a   (6)

(too)   c h o f a t o o i e d i d t o o f o r l i e n o t t o o e s a t o o o n l i e t o t o o i e s   (5)

(who)   h o w t h e n a t a r e w h o m n a r e w h o z c a b e w h o i t y u w h o n g h o w a   (4)

Part 3

The words in the first column have endings.
Write the same words without endings in the second column.

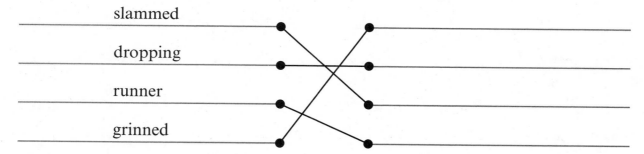

slammed

dropping

runner

grinned

Part 4

Copy the sentence.

The fat rat ate oats for seven days.

_____

Writing words, finding words, suffixes, copying sentences

Name _____

Part 5

The Rat That Had a Fast Rate

Sandy had a rat that ate fast. She said, "That rat eats too	13
much. I must make the rat slow down."	21
Sandy went to the store and got ten packs of gum. She	33
said, "I will smear the gum on the oats." Then she gave the oats	47
to the rat. "Here are some oats," she said. "You will have fun	60
eating them."	62
The rat began eating at a very fast rate. But then the rate	75
began to go down.	79
The rat chomped and chomped. The rat said, "I like oats,	90
but these oats are not fun. I am chomping as fast as I can, but	105
the oats don't go down."	110
Sandy said, "Ho, ho. There is gum on them so that you can	123
not eat at a fast rate."	129
The rat said, "Give me the oats that do not have gum on	142
them, and I will eat slowly."	148
Sandy said, "I am happy to hear that."	156
She gave the rat oats that did not have gum on them. The	169
rat did 2 things. She bit Sandy's hand. Then she ate the oats at a	184
very fast rate.	187
Sandy said, "You little rat. You told me a lie."	197

A Note to the Parent

Listen to the student read the passage. Count the number of words read in one minute and the number of errors.

Number of words read _____   Number of errors _____

We read the story _____ times.

(Parent's/Listener's) signature _____

Date _____

Reading fluency

Name _____

Part 1

Copy the sentences.

The camp woman gave him a hammer.

_____

She fixed the lamp.

_____

Can you work better than the rest of us?

_____

Part 2

The words in the first column have endings.
Write the same words without endings in the second column.

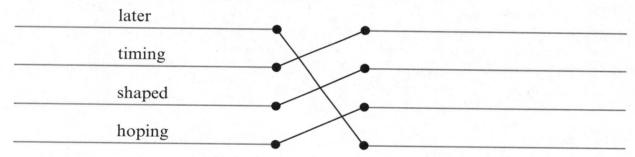

later

timing

shaped

hoping

Part 3

(oa)   a s w h e b t o e a h e a o a h e a t o a d o o a e a o l o a r e e s t o a e r u w f o a i ⑥

(for)   f i l l f o r f e e d s f o r t o r n f o r t o o f s a t f o r l i e a t o f o f i s ④

(make) h o w t h e m a k e m a d w h o m a k e h o w m a k e m a d e i t m a k e m a n s ④

Copying sentences, suffixes, finding words

Name _____

Part 4

Sandy's Plan for the Rat's Fast Rate

Sandy's rat ate at a fast rate. The rat ran at a fast rate. And	15
it even hopped at a fast rate. Sandy had a plan to make the rat's	30
rate go down.	33
Sandy got a rat that did not eat at a fast rate and did not	48
run fast. This rat was fat. It sat and sat. When this rat ate, it	63
chomped slowly. Sandy said, "I will take this slow rat and show	75
my fast rat how to be slow." Sandy dropped the fat rat into the	89
box with the fast rat.	94
The fast rat said, "This fat rat needs help. It is too fat. I will	109
show it how to go fast."	115
Sandy's rat bit the fat rat on the nose. "Stop that," he said.	128
Sandy's rat said, "Make me stop."	134
The fat rat began to run after Sandy's rat. These rats ran	146
and ran and ran. Then the fat rat said, "I must rest. I need to	161
eat some oats."	164
Sandy's rat said, "If you don't eat fast, I will eat these oats	177
and then no oats will be left for you."	186
"No," the fat rat said. "I can eat as fast as the next rat." And	201
it did.	203

A Note to the Parent Listen to the student read the passage. Count the number of words read in one minute and the number of errors.

Number of words read _____   Number of errors _____

We read the story _____ times.

(Parent's/Listener's) signature _____

Date _____

Reading fluency

Name _____

Part 1
The words in the first column have endings.
Write the same words without endings in the second column.

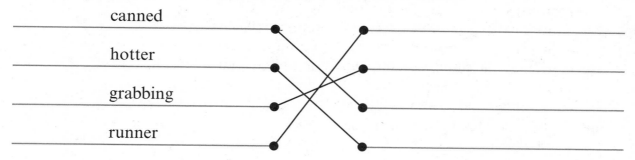

canned

hotter

grabbing

runner

Part 2
Copy the sentences.

The man with the faster rate will win.

_____

I can even take a bath faster than you.

_____

Part 3
Match the words and complete them.

their   ld

women   th

held   sh

show   men

Part 4

(day)   a s d a d d a y b a d d a y a t b i d d i d o n d e e r d a y a f t e r d a y d e n ④

(bath) b a c k b a t h b a g b i t p a t h b a t h f o r b e a t s a t f o r b e d b a t h b r ③

(soon) h o w t h e s o o n t o o s o o n r o o m o f m a k e s o o n b r o o m s o o n s ④

Suffixes, copying sentences, writing words, finding words

Part 5

Champ at the Camp

A man named Champ went down a road. He came to a	12
camp. He stopped and said, "I hate to work, but I need to eat.	26
So I will see if I can get a job at this camp." So Champ went to	43
the woman who ran the camp. Champ said, "Can I work at this	56
camp? I can do lots of jobs here."	64
The camp woman said, "Are you a tramp?"	72
Champ said, "No, I am a champ at camp work."	82
"Can you fix lamps?"	86
"Yes," Champ said.	89
"Can you make boat ramps?"	94
"Yes," said Champ. "I am the champ at ramps."	103
The camp woman said, "Then I will let you work at this	115
camp." The camp woman gave Champ a hammer. She said,	125
"Take this hammer and make a ramp for these boats."	135
Champ got boards and began to hammer. When the sun	145
went down, he had made the boat ramp. He said, "Now I have	158
to eat."	160
But the woman from the camp did not let Champ rest. She	172
handed Champ a broken lamp. Then she said, "Take these	182
clamps and fix this lamp."	187
So Champ got a clamp to hold the lamp. He fixed the lamp.	200

A Note to the Parent   Listen to the student read the passage. Count the number of words read in one minute and the number of errors.

Number of words read _____   Number of errors _____

We read the story _____ times.

(Parent's/Listener's) signature _____

Date _____

Reading fluency

Part 1

The words in the first column have endings.
Write the same words without endings in the second column.

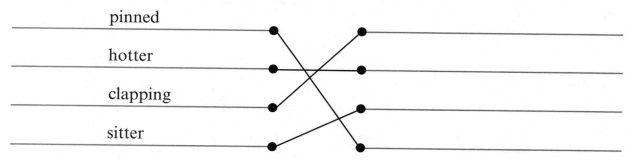

pinned _____

hotter _____

clapping _____

sitter _____

Part 2

Read the sentences in the box.

| 1. Champ said, "I am your brother." |
| 2. He said, "You need boaters." |
| 3. The camp woman clapped. |

Write the last word of these sentences.

2nd sentence _____

1st sentence _____

3rd sentence _____

Part 3

Match the words and complete them.

smell _____   •   •   eer

stand _____   •   •   ell

cheer _____   •   •   th

bath _____   •   •   and

Part 4

Copy the sentences.

The camp woman held her nose.

_____

Bob bent down and began to paddle.

_____

Suffixes, writing words, writing sentences

Name _____

Part 5

Champ Has a Meet with Sam

Champ slept at the table. The next day he woke up and felt	13
rested. He went to the woman who ran the camp. The woman held	26
her nose as she said, "You smell, Champ. Will you take a bath?"	39
"No," Champ said.	42
Just then, a big man named Sam came up. He held his nose	55
and said, "Champ, you are not the champ worker at this camp.	67
I am."	69
A woman said, "Let's have a meet between Champ and Sam."	80
So the men and women set things up for the big meet. They	93
gave a tamping pole to each man. They said, "We will see how	106
well Champ can tamp."	110
They went to the hill. The camp woman said, "Take these	121
tamping poles and see how fast you can pound the ruts from	133
this path."	135
Sam and Champ began tamping. They tamped the path for	145
three miles. Sam was a very fast tamper. But Champ tamped	156
faster. The men and women did not cheer for Champ. They	167
said, "Champ can tamp fast, but Sam can make ramps faster	178
than Champ can."	181
So Champ and Sam went to the lake. The camp woman	192
said, "Each man will clamp seventy boards and hammer the	202
boards on a frame."	206

A Note to the Parent   Listen to the student read the passage. Count the number of words read in one minute and the number of errors.

Number of words read _____   Number of errors _____

We read the story _____ times.

(Parent's/Listener's) signature _____

Date _____

Reading fluency

Name _____

Part 1

Read the item and fill in the circle next to the answer.
Write the answer in the blank.

1. Champ said, "I can not open this door. This door has a _____ on it."
   ○ handle   ○ note   ○ lock   ○ top

2. Big Bob said, "I will _____ the door in."
   ○ fix   ○ kick   ○ pick   ○ lock

3. The old man held a _____ to his ear.
   ○ pick   ○ handle   ○ horn   ○ top

4. Big Bob said, "Make a _____ for the old man."
   ○ clock   ○ lock   ○ horn   ○ note

Part 2

The words in the first column have endings.
Write the same words without endings in the second column.

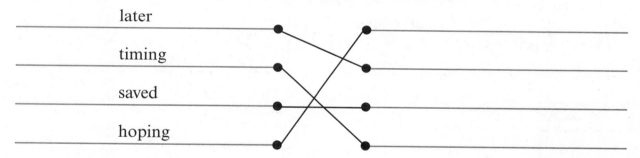

later

timing

saved

hoping

Part 3

Copy the sentences.

Champ grabbed the handle of the door.

_____

The old man hit the lock with a hammer.

_____

Directions, Part 1: Read the directions to the student. "Read the item and fill in the circle next to the answer. Write the answer in the blank."

Name _____

Part 4

Champ's Brother Has a Boat Meet

One day a man came to the camp. This man was big and fat.	14
He smelled as bad as a goat. He went up to the camp woman	28
and said, "My name is Bob. I do not like to work, but I have to	44
eat. And I am the best worker you have seen."	54
Champ, who was champ of the camp, went up to the camp	66
woman and said, "That is Big Bob, my brother."	75
Big Bob said, "No. You can't be my brother. My brother is	87
fat, and he smells. But you are not fat, and you do not smell."	101
Champ said, "But I am your brother."	108
The camp woman said, "We do not need more workers in	119
this camp."	121
Champ said, "But you need boaters. And Big Bob is the	132
best there is."	135
The camp woman held her nose. She said, "We will see how	147
well Big Bob can do in a boat meet with Sam."	158
Each man got in a boat. But Big Bob had an old boat that	172
was very slow.	175
The camp woman said, "When I clap, begin paddling.	184
Paddle as fast as you can to the other shore of the lake."	197
The camp woman clapped, and the men began to paddle.	207

A Note to the Parent — Listen to the student read the passage. Count the number of words read in one minute and the number of errors.

Number of words read _____ Number of errors _____

We read the story _____ times.

(Parent's/Listener's) signature _____

Date _____

Reading fluency

Part 1

Read the item and fill in the circle next to the answer.
Write the answer in the blank.

1. The con man had a box of _____.

   ○ locks   ○ clocks   ○ mops   ○ tops

2. Champ was a fast _____ raker.

   ○ slope   ○ slop   ○ shore   ○ shop

3. Champ said, "I will _____ this mop near the door."

   ○ prop   ○ slop   ○ stop   ○ bop

4. The con man sold the camp woman _____ mops.

   ○ seven   ○ thin   ○ 50   ○ bad

Part 2

The words in the first column have endings.
Write the same words without endings in the second column.

_____ mopping ●————————● _____

_____ grabbed ●   ● _____

_____ dropper ●   ✕   ● _____

_____ slipping ●————————● _____

Part 3

Copy the sentence.

The con man was glad to sell the mops.

_____

Comprehension items, suffixes, copying sentences

Part 4

The Clock Maker at the Camp

Champ and his brother Big Bob went to the shed. Champ	11
grabbed the handle of the door. He said, "This door has a	23
lock on it. How will we get in this shed? The hammers and the	37
tamping poles are in here. We need hammers and tampers if we	49
are to work."	52
Big Bob said, "Brother, don't bother with that lock. I will kick	64
the door in."	67
"No," Champ said. "Let's go to the camp woman and see if	79
she can get in this shed."	85
So they went to the camp woman. She said, "I will get a	98
man to fix that lock."	103
Later, an old man came to the camp. He had a big bag and	117
a big horn that he held to his ear.	126
He said, "I am here to fix a clock."	135
The men said, "We do not need someone to fix a clock. We	148
need someone to fix a lock. We cannot get in the shed because	161
the door is locked."	165
The old man said, "You say the door is clocked?"	175
Big Bob said, "Make a note for the old man. Even with his	188
ear horn, he cannot hear."	193
So Champ got a pen and made a note.	202

A Note to the Parent

Listen to the student read the passage. Count the number of words read in one minute and the number of errors.

Number of words read _____   Number of errors _____

We read the story _____ times.

(Parent's/Listener's) signature _____

Date _____

Reading fluency

Part 1

Match the words and complete them.

matter	cause
because	ck
lifted	ed
shack	mat

Part 2

Copy the sentences.

Cathy worked in a dress shop.

_____

Cathy and Pam left the shed and sat on a bench.

_____

Part 3

Read the item and fill in the circle next to the answer.
Write the answer in the blank.

1. Pam led Cathy to a _____.
   ○ dress shop   ○ big camp   ○ clock store   ○ fish shed

2. The man in a big coat said, "I am a _____."
   ○ cook   ○ worker   ○ fish packer   ○ slop raker

3. The man had a basket of fish in his _____.
   ○ shed   ○ boat   ○ shop   ○ store

4. The man in the fish shed gave Pam and Cathy _____ chips.
   ○ free   ○ five   ○ fish   ○ flat

Writing words, copying sentences, comprehension items

Name _____

Part 4

Champ Meets the Con Man

A con man came to the camp. That con man came up the	13
camp road with a box. The camp woman met him.	23
The con man dropped his box and held the lid up. He	35
grabbed a mop from the box. He said, "The workers will like	47
this mop. It is fatter than other mops. So a worker can mop	60
faster with this mop."	64
The camp woman said, "I will get someone to take that	75
mop and see how well it works." So the camp woman yelled for	88
Champ.	89
Champ was on a slope near a shore of the lake. Was he	102
making a ramp? No, he was raking slop near the pond. He was	115
a fast slop raker. He went to the con man and the camp woman.	129
The camp woman handed the mop to Champ.	137
"Here," she said. "See if this fatter mop mops faster than	148
other mops."	150
Champ said, "I hate to stop slopping to do some mopping."	161
The camp woman said, "When I say that you must mop,	172
you must mop. So take this fat mop and begin mopping."	183
But Champ did not begin mopping. He went to the eating	194
table and said, "I will prop this mop near the door, and I will	208
sit."	209

A Note to the Parent

Listen to the student read the passage. Count the number of words read in one minute and the number of errors.

Number of words read _____ Number of errors _____

We read the story _____ times.

(Parent's/Listener's) signature _____

Date _____

Reading fluency

Part 1

The words in the first column have endings.
Write the same words without endings in the second column.

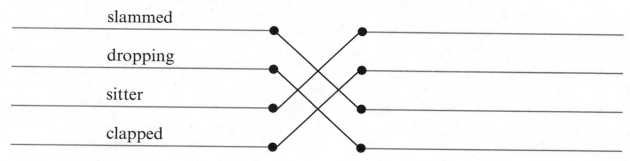

slammed

dropping

sitter

clapped

Part 2

Read the sentence and fill in the circle next to the answer.
Write the answer in the blank.

1. When Gretta said, "Ho, ho," Chee _____.

   ◯ made a note   ◯ sat near the door   ◯ became very mad

2. Chee asked Gretta, "Did you _____ at your job?"

   ◯ work fast   ◯ feel sad   ◯ have fun   ◯ sell fish

Part 3

Copy the sentences.

She got better and better at saying things.

_____

I don't like to stay at home.

_____

He will get a job, too.

_____

Suffixes, comprehension items, copying sentences

Part 4

Cathy and a Band at the Bend

Cathy worked in a dress shop. One day she said, "I need a	13
rest." So she went to her pal, Pam. She said, "Pam, let us go	27
to hear a band play. A band is near the bend in the road. They	42
play well."	44
Then Cathy and Pam went to hear the band. When they	55
got near the bend in the road, Pam said, "I need to eat. Let me	70
lead you to a little shed. It is near the stream. They sell fish and	85
chips in that shed."	89
So Pam led Cathy to the fish shed near the stream. The	101
shack was packed with folks. The folks were yelling, "I was	112
next. Give me my order of fish and chips."	121
Pam said, "This is a mess."	127
Cathy and Pam left the fish shed and sat on a bench. A man	141
came up to them. He had a net, and he was dressed in a big	156
coat. He set the net in the sand, and then he sat down on the	171
bench. He asked Cathy, "What is the matter?"	179
Cathy said, "The shed is packed. We will be late to hear the	192
band."	193
The man said, "I am a fish packer. If you need fish, let me	207
help you."	209

A Note to the Parent Listen to the student read the passage. Count the number of words read in one minute and the number of errors.

Number of words read _____ Number of errors _____

We read the story _____ times.

(Parent's/Listener's) signature _____

Date _____

Reading fluency

Part 1

The words in the first column have endings.
Write the same words without endings in the second column.

trades _____

liked _____

saving _____

maker _____

Part 2

Read the item and fill in the circle next to the answer.
Write the answer in the blank.

1. The clock maker did not _____ well.

   ○ see   ○ read   ○ hear   ○ feel

2. The con man said, "We will _____ in the shade."

   ○ stay   ○ sit   ○ play   ○ work

3. The clock maker said, "I will not _____ this horn."

   ○ sell   ○ play   ○ pack   ○ trade

4. The clock maker handed his _____ to the con man.

   ○ little horn   ○ corn   ○ big horn   ○ pack

Part 3

Copy the sentences.

The con man dressed up like a corn grower.

_____

He stamped up and down.

_____

Suffixes, comprehension items, copying sentences

Name _____

Part 4

Chee, the Dog

Gretta got a little dog. She named the dog Chee. Chee got	12
bigger and bigger each day.	17
On a very cold day, Gretta said, "Chee, I must go to the	30
store. You stay home. I will be back."	38
Chee said, "Store, lots, of, for, no."	45
Then Gretta said, "Did I hear that dog say things?"	55
Chee said, "Say things can I do."	62
Gretta said, "Dogs don't say things. So I must not hear	73
well."	74
But Chee did say things. Gretta left the dog at home. When	86
Gretta came back, Chee was sitting near the door.	95
Gretta said, "That dog is bigger than she was."	104
Then the dog said, "Read, read for me of left."	114
Gretta said, "Is that dog saying that she can read?" Gretta	125
got a pad and made a note for the dog. The note said, "Dear	139
Chee, if you can read this note, I will hand you a bag of bones."	154
Gretta said, "Let's see if you can read."	162
Chee said, "Dear Chee, if you can read this note, I will ham	175
you a bag for beans."	180
Gretta said, "She can read, but she can't read well. Ho, ho."	192
Chee became very mad. She said, "For note don't read ho ho."	204

A Note to the Parent

Listen to the student read the passage. Count the number of words read in one minute and the number of errors.

Number of words read _____   Number of errors _____

We read the story _____ times.

(Parent's/Listener's) signature _____

Date _____

Reading fluency

Part 1

Match the words and complete them.

felt ——————●	●—————— ft
help ——————●	●—————— se
left ——————●	●—————— lt
self ——————●	●—————— he

Part 2

Copy the sentences.

Chee began to say odd things.

_____

She left her home to get a job.

_____

He had tears on his cheeks.

_____

The man came back with his boss.

_____

Part 3

The words in the first column have endings.
Write the same words without endings in the second column.

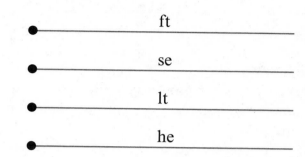

getting

dropper

grabbed

bigger

Writing words, copying sentences, inflectional suffixes

Name _____

Part 4

The Old Clock Maker and the Con Man

The old clock maker did not hear well. He left the camp	12
with the lock. He had this lock in his pack. He went down a	26
road from the camp. Then he met a corn grower.	36
But the corn grower was not a corn grower. He was the con	49
man dressed up like a corn grower. That con man liked conning	61
folks.	62
The con man said, "Let's go sit in the shade near my shed."	75
"Yes," the clock maker said, "I will trade for a bed."	86
"No, not a bed," the con man said. "Shed. We will sit near	99
my shed."	101
The clock maker said, "Yes, I like a sled, but I don't see a	115
sled."	116
The con man was mad at the clock maker. He yelled, "WE	128
WILL SIT IN THE SHADE."	133
"Yes," the clock maker said. "I am ready to trade."	143
The con man led the clock maker to the shade. He held the	156
clock maker's horn to the clock maker's ear. Then he said, "Will	168
you trade your pack for some corn?"	175
"No," the clock maker said, "I need this horn. So I will not	188
trade this horn. But I will trade my pack for corn."	199
The con man got a sack of corn.	207

A Note to the Parent Listen to the student read the passage. Count the number of words read in one minute and the number of errors.

Number of words read _____ Number of errors _____

We read the story _____ times.

(Parent's/Listener's) signature _____

Date _____

Reading fluency

Part 1

Read the words in the box. Then fill in the blanks.

worked	well	rode	named	fast
good	best	swam	ran	bent

There was a ranch in the West. The rancher who _____ this ranch was

_____ Emma Branch. She rode a horse _____. She chopped

_____, and she swam faster. The men and women who _____ for

Emma Branch liked her. They said, "She is the best in the West."

Part 2

The words in the first column have endings.
Write the same words without endings in the second column.

named

timer

cones

saving

Part 3

Copy the sentences.

She checked up on the workers.

_____

Get ready to leave now.

_____

This horse is very tame.

_____

Vocabulary/context clues, suffixes, copying sentences

Part 4

Chee Goes for a Job

Chee felt sad. So she left her home to get a job.	12
Chee went to a fire station. She went up to the man who ran	26
the station and said, "I need a job. Can you help me?"	38
The man said, "Is my hearing going bad, or did that dog say	51
something to me?"	54
The dog said, "I did say something. Do you have a job for	67
me?"	68
The man said, "Ho, ho. That dog is saying things, but dogs	80
can't speak."	82
Chee got so mad that she began to say odd things. "Fire	94
station for of to go," she said.	101
The man said, "Ho, ho. This dog is fun. I will keep this dog	115
with me. I like to hear the odd things that dog can say."	128
Chee was so mad at the fireman she said, "From of for,	140
fireman."	141
The fireman fell down and went, "Ho, ho, ho." He had tears	153
on his cheeks. His ears got red. Then he patted Chee and said,	166
"I didn't mean to make you mad. But you do say odd things."	179
Then the dog said to herself, "I will not work here. I can't	192
stand to hear that fireman go 'Ho, ho.'"	200

A Note to the Parent Listen to the student read the passage. Count the number of words read in one minute and the number of errors.

Number of words read _____ Number of errors _____

We read the story _____ times.

(Parent's/Listener's) signature _____

Date _____

Reading fluency

Name _____

Part 1
Read the words in the box. Then fill in the blanks.

fastest	packer	stick	plant	old
stackers	slowest	odd	mad	slate
pack	made	slat	job	stack

Chee got a _____ at a _____ plant. When she was not

_____, she did not say _____ things. The woman who ran the

_____ showed Chee how to _____ slate. At the end of one year,

Chee was one of the fastest _____.

Part 2
Copy the sentences.

The woman showed Chee how to stack slate.

_____

She worked at the plant for nearly a year.

_____

Set that slab on top of the pile.

_____

Part 3
The words in the first column have endings.
Write the same words without endings in the second column.

clapped

running

swimmer

biggest

Vocabulary/context clues, copying sentences, suffixes

Part 4

The Rancher

There was a big ranch in the West. The rancher who ran this	13
ranch was named Emma Branch. She rode a horse well. She	24
chopped fast, and she swam faster. The men and women who	35
worked for Emma Branch liked her. They said, "She is the best	47
in the West." On her ranch she had sheep, and she had cows.	60
There were goats and horses. There was a lot of grass.	71
The rancher had a lot of women and men working for her.	83
They worked with the sheep and the goats, and they milked the	95
cows. Each worker had a horse. But the rancher's horse was the	107
biggest and the best. It was a big, black horse named Flop.	119
Flop got its name because it reared up. When Flop reared	130
up, any rider on it fell down and went "flop" in the grass. But	144
Flop did not rear up when the rancher rode it. Emma Branch	156
bent near Flop's ear and said, "Let's go, Flop." And they went.	168
She did not have to slap the horse. She didn't have to jab her	182
heels and yell at Flop. She just said, "Let's go," and they went	195
like a shot.	198
Every day, she checked up on the workers to see what they	210
were doing.	212

A Note to the Parent

Listen to the student read the passage. Count the number of words read in one minute and the number of errors.

Number of words read _____ Number of errors _____

We read the story _____ times.

(Parent's/Listener's) signature _____

Date _____

Reading fluency

Name _____

Part 1

Read the words in the box. Then fill in the blanks.

leave	shop	sheep	sacks	best
steal	work	shave	plan	faster
packs	shears	wool	well	fake

The con man said, "I can _____ a sheep before it sees the

_____. You can _____, but you cannot get someone who

can shave _____ than me."

The con man told the rancher to get him ten _____ for holding the

_____. He did not plan to shear _____. He planned to

_____ them.

Part 2

Match the words and complete them.

before •   • est

steal •   • st

still •   • eal

chest •   • fore

Part 3

Copy the sentences.

He got the shears from his pack.

_____

He planned to pack sheep into sacks.

_____

The rancher sat on the con man and shaved his locks.

_____

Vocabulary/context clues, writing words, copying sentences

Part 4

Chee Stacks Slate

Chee went to get a job, but no plant had jobs for dogs that	14
say things. At last, Chee went to a slate plant. Chee said, "I	27
hope that I can get a job here." Chee went into the plant. Chee	41
went past stacks of slate. She came to the woman who ran the	54
plant. Chee asked, "Do you have a job I can do in this plant?"	68
The woman looked at Chee. Then the woman said, "Ho, ho,	79
ho. I cannot help going 'Ho, ho, ho.' "	87
Chee got so mad that she began to say odd things. "Stop	99
slate for from me, of go so no to do, ho ho."	111
The woman fell down and kept going "Ho, ho, ho."	121
Chee felt so mad that she did not stop saying odd things.	133
The woman got sore from going "Ho, ho." She had lots of	145
tears on her cheeks. Then she stopped ho-hoing and said, "I	156
have seen lots of things, but I have never seen a dog that said	170
odd things."	172
Chee was not so mad now. So Chee began to say things that	185
made sense. Chee said, "I told you not to go 'Ho, ho.' I told you	200
that I need a job."	205

A Note to the Parent

Listen to the student read the passage. Count the number of words read in one minute and the number of errors.

Number of words read _____ Number of errors _____

We read the story _____ times.

(Parent's/Listener's) signature _____

Date _____

Reading fluency

Name _____

Part 1

Read the words in the box. Then fill in the blanks.

tamps	ranch	rest	pack	old
odd	slop	camp	say	stay
sack	ramps	hill	lake	leave

Champ worked at the _____ for nearly a year. He tamped and made

_____.

Now he said, "I will _____ this camp. Champs don't _____

in a camp for more than a year."

So Champ got his _____. He told the camp woman, "The work here is

getting _____, and I need a _____."

Part 2

The words in the first column have endings.
Write the same words without endings in the second column.

_____ maker

_____ ropes

_____ shaved

_____ riding

Part 3

Copy the sentences.

He worked there for nearly a year.

_____

When the sun comes up, he will shear sheep.

_____

Vocabulary/context clues, suffixes, copying sentences

Name _____

Part 4

The Con Man and the Sheep Rancher

Emma Branch had a lot of big sheep on her ranch. One	12
day she said, "My sheep need shearing. I will send for a sheep	25
shearer."	26
So she told one of her helpers to go to town and get	39
someone who can shear sheep. The helper went down the road	50
to town. But he did not get there. He met the con man on the	65
road. The con man said, "Where are you going?"	74
The helper said, "The rancher needs her sheep sheared."	83
The con man said, "I am the best at shearing sheep. I have	96
shears in my pack."	100
So Emma's helper led the con man back to the ranch. When	112
they got there, Emma yelled from the door, "I hope that man	124
can shear fast."	127
The con man said, "I can shave sheep. I can shape. And I	140
can shear."	142
"But how is your rate at shearing?" the rancher asked.	152
"I can go so fast that I can shave a sheep before it sees the	167
shears. You can shop and shop, but you cannot get someone	178
who can shape or shave faster than me."	186
So the con man got the job. He told the rancher to get him	200
ten sacks for holding the wool.	206

A Note to the Parent

Listen to the student read the passage. Count the number of words read in one minute and the number of errors.

Number of words read _____ Number of errors _____

We read the story _____ times.

(Parent's/Listener's) signature _____

Date _____

Reading fluency

Part 1

Read the item and fill in the circle next to the answer.
Write the answer in the blank.

1. Champ was sleeping near a sheep _____.

   ○ camp   ○ shed   ○ shop   ○ ranch

2. Champ felt more like _____ than shearing.

   ○ sweeping   ○ shaving   ○ yelling   ○ sleeping

3. Emma said, "You have _____ minutes to shear _____ sheep."

   ○ five   ○ 50   ○ 20   ○ ten

4. Emma kept her _____ with Champ.

   ○ plan   ○ ranch   ○ deal   ○ hand

Part 2

Copy the sentences.

The sun came up in the morning.

_____

The cook will make a good meal.

_____

Part 3

The words in the first column have endings.
Write the same words without endings in the second column.

sweeping	
reached	
helper	

Comprehension items, copying sentences, suffixes

Name _____

Part 4

The Rancher and Champ

Champ had worked at the camp for nearly a year. He had	12
tamped and made ramps. He had fixed lamps and raked slop	23
near the lake. But now he said, "I think I will leave this camp. I	38
am a champ, and champs don't stay in the same camp for more	51
than a year."	54
So Champ got his pack and went to the camp woman. He	66
told her, "I must go now. The work here is getting old, and I	80
need a rest. I will go sit in the shade and eat beans and rest. It is	97
time to go where I do not have to take a bath."	109
So Champ left and went down the camp road. When he got	121
to a town, he said, "I see a person on a big black horse. I will	137
ask that rider where I can go to rest in the shade." Champ went	151
up to the person on the black horse and said, "Tell me, where	164
can I go to rest in the shade?"	172
The person on the horse was Emma Branch. She was the	183
rancher that shaved the con man. She said, "I help men and	195
women who work well."	199
"I work well," Champ said.	204

A Note to the Parent

Listen to the student read the passage. Count the number of words read in one minute and the number of errors.

Number of words read _____ Number of errors _____

We read the story _____ times.

(Parent's/Listener's) signature _____

Date _____

Reading fluency

Copyright © SRA/McGraw-Hill. Permission is granted to reproduce for classroom use.

Name _____

Part 1

Match the words and complete them.

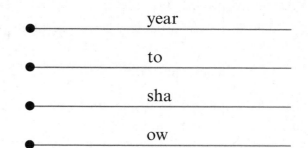

slow   year

shame   to

town   sha

yearly   ow

Part 2

Copy the sentences.

He got slower and slower with each meal that he ate.

_____

Emma went to town and bragged.

_____

Part 3

Read the words in the box. Then fill in the blanks.

like	rested	said	mean	time
best	look	shave	shape	shade
bad	meet	good	neat	seem

The rancher said, "We will have the _____ at the end of this week. So get

in _____."

"Yes, yes," the fat champ said.

"I _____ it," the rancher said. "You _____ to be in

_____ shape. You have _____ for seven weeks. Now you don't

_____ like you can do things very fast."

Writing words, copying sentences, vocabulary/context clues

Part 4

Champ Shows the Rancher How to Shear

The sun came up in the morning. Champ was sleeping near	11
a big sheep shed. The rancher's helper came to wake him up.	23
Champ said, "Leave me be. I am sleeping." So Champ went	34
back to sleep.	37
The helper ran to Emma and said, "That Champ didn't get	48
up when I went to wake him up."	56
Emma grabbed shears and ran over to Champ. Her helper	66
ran with her. When they got to Champ, the rancher handed her	78
shears to her helper. She said to Champ, "If you don't get up,	91
my helper will give you a shearing."	98
So Champ got up and went to the sheep shed with Emma.	110
Emma said, "We have a deal. If you can shear 50 sheep as	123
fast as you hammer, you may stay and rest on my ranch."	135
Then she handed the shears to Champ. Champ felt more	145
like sleeping than shearing. He said, "I did not sleep well. When	157
I am not rested, I cannot work well. I will have to jump up and	172
down to wake up." So Champ began to jump up and down.	184
Then he said, "Now I can shear sheep."	192
"Good," Emma said. "You have 50 minutes to shear 50	202
sheep."	203

A Note to the Parent

Listen to the student read the passage. Count the number of words read in one minute and the number of errors.

Number of words read _____ Number of errors _____

We read the story _____ times.

(Parent's/Listener's) signature _____

Date _____

Reading fluency

Name _____

Part 1

Read the item and fill in the circle next to the answer.
Write the answer in the blank.

1. Shelly made a _____ of wool as big as a hill.
   ○ pack   ○ sheer   ○ heap   ○ sweep

2. Champ made a pile of wool as big as a _____ sheep.
   ○ little   ○ fatter   ○ big   ○ short

3. Emma said to Champ, "You will _____ like a horse."
   ○ run   ○ go   ○ rest   ○ work

4. Champ had never been _____ in a meet before.
   ○ shaved   ○ beaten   ○ broken   ○ picked

Part 2

The words in the first column have endings.
Write the same words without endings in the second column.

_____ melted
_____ working
_____ beaten
_____ slower

Part 3

Copy the sentences.

She showed the others how fast she was.

_____

He ate big meals of ham and beans.

_____

Comprehension items, inflectional suffixes, copying sentences

Part 4

The Rancher Sets Up a Shearing Meet

Champ had stayed at the ranch for seven weeks. Every day,	11
he had big meals of beef and ham and beans and corn. Every	24
day, he sat in the shade near the lake. And every day, he got a	39
little slower. He got slower and slower with each meal that he	51
ate.	52
The rancher did not think that Champ was slow. She had	63
seen him go so fast that the helper did not sweep the wool as	77
fast as Champ shaved sheep.	82
Emma went to town and bragged. She said, "There is a man	94
on my ranch who can shear sheep faster than anyone you have	106
seen."	107
When Emma was in town one day, she told a lot of people,	120
"A man on my ranch can beat anyone in a shearing meet."	132
A woman named Shelly stepped up to Emma and said, "I	143
think I can beat anyone in a shearing meet."	152
"Let's have a meet," the others yelled.	159
"Yes," the rancher said.	163
So they set up a meet between Champ and Shelly. A man	175
said, "Let's make bets. I will bet on Shelly. I have seen her work	189
with shears, and I think she can beat any other worker."	200

A Note to the Parent

Listen to the student read the passage. Count the number of words read in one minute and the number of errors.

Number of words read _____ Number of errors _____

We read the story _____ times.

(Parent's/Listener's) signature _____

Date _____

Reading fluency

Part 1

The words in the first column have endings.
Write the same words without endings in the second column.

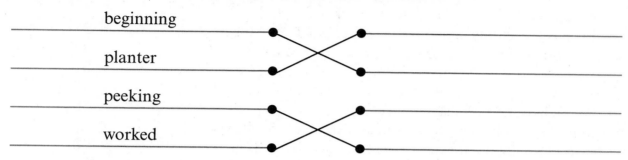

beginning

planter

peeking

worked

Part 2

Read the words in the box. Then fill in the blanks.

shaping	shaving	faster	week	work
fatter	sore	sheared	hot	meals
cold	hands	hammer	made	shape

The rancher gave Champ more work. At the end of the day, Champ was

_____.

But at the end of the week, he began to get _____. His _____

began to go like a flash. His shears began to get _____ when he was

_____ sheep. Champ was beginning to get back in _____.

Part 3

Copy the sentences.

His hammer began to go like a flash.

_____

There was no more work at the ranch.

_____

Suffixes, vocabulary/context clues, copying sentences

Part 4

The Shearing Meet

The rancher had told Champ to get in shape for the	11
shearing meet. But did Champ get in shape? No. He ate big	23
meals of corn and ham and beans and meat. Then he went to	36
sleep.	37
Was Champ in shape at the end of the week? No. Champ	49
was out of shape and very slow.	56
People from town came to the ranch with Shelly. Shelly was	67
in tip-top shape. Before the meet began, she sheared a sheep to	79
show the others how fast she was. Before the wool that fell from	92
the sheep had landed, that sheep was shaved from one end to	104
the other.	106
The people cheered. "Shelly can beat anyone at shearing,"	115
they yelled.	117
Champ had to work to pick up the shears. He said, "I may	130
have rested too much, but when I get going, I will speed up."	143
The rancher said, "Shelly and Champ will shear all day."	153
Champ said to his helper, "I hope you are fast at sweeping.	165
This wool will be dropping very fast."	172
The rancher said, "Go," and the shearing began.	180
Champ's shears did not go like a flash. And the wool did	192
not pile up fast. "I must go faster," he said.	202

A Note to the Parent

Listen to the student read the passage. Count the number of words read in one minute and the number of errors.

Number of words read _____   Number of errors _____

We read the story _____ times.

(Parent's/Listener's) signature _____

Date _____

Reading fluency

Part 1

Read the item and fill in the circle next to the answer.
Write the answer in the blank.

1. Shelly said, "I have never been _____ in a shearing meet."

   ◯ broken   ◯ cheered   ◯ beaten   ◯ shaved

2. At the end of the meet, Champ had sheared _____ sheep.

   ◯ 5,000   ◯ 9,000   ◯ 210   ◯ 501

3. Shelly had sheared _____ sheep.

   ◯ 5,000   ◯ 9,000   ◯ 210   ◯ 501

Part 2

The words in the first column have endings.
Write the same words without endings in the second column.

_____ cheered
_____ panting
_____ beaten
_____ rancher

Part 3

Copy the sentences.

She is the best worker at the plant.

_____

The people from town waved to Champ.

_____

Her helpers began to bag the wool.

_____

Comprehension items, suffixes, copying sentences

Part 4

Champ Gets in Shape

Champ worked and worked at the ranch. Every day, he got
up when the sun was peeking over the hill in the east. Champ
did not eat a big meal. He went to the sheep shed and sheared
sheep. Then he picked corn. Then he ate a little meal. He had
an egg and a little bit of ham. He said, "I need more to eat."

"No more," the rancher said. "Back to work for you." She
handed Champ a hammer. "Take boards and make a gate," she
said.

After Champ had made a gate, the rancher said, "Now take
boards and make a pen for goats." After Champ had made a
pen of boards, she said, "Next, you're going to dig holes for
planting trees."

So Champ dug ten tree holes. Then he planted three trees.
Then he sheared more sheep. At last, the rancher said, "Now
you may eat a meal."

But it was a very little meal. Champ ate it and said, "I need
more to eat."

"No more," she said. And she gave Champ more work.

At the end of the day, Champ was sore. He was sore the
next day.

But at the end of the week, he began to get faster.

11
24
38
51
66
77
88
89
100
112
124
126
137
148
153
167
170
180
193
195
207

**A Note
to the Parent**

Listen to the student read the passage. Count the number of words
read in one minute and the number of errors.

Number of words read _____ Number of errors _____

We read the story _____ times.

(Parent's/Listener's) signature _____

Date _____

Reading fluency

Name _____

Part 1

Read the words in the box. Then fill in the blanks.

day	packer	speed	rate	packing	plant
quit	week	stacking	year	shearing	rat
stacker	shack	leave	slacks	sick	time

Chee worked as a slate _____ for nearly a year. By then, her

_____ of _____ was very good. But she was getting a little

_____ of her job. "Stack, stack, stack," she said. "It's time to do something

else." So she went to the woman who ran the slate _____ and said, "I think I

have to _____ and get another job."

Part 2

The words in the first column have endings.
Write the same words without endings in the second column.

_____ waited

_____ stacker

_____ seated

_____ nearly

Part 3

Match the words and complete them.

_____ something   •   •   some

_____ person   •   •   low

_____ yellow   •   •   ts

_____ coats   •   •   son

Vocabulary/context, inflectional suffixes, writing words

Part 4

The Meet with Shelly Is Set

Champ felt he was in shape for the shearing meet. When	11
there was no more work on Emma's ranch, Champ did some	22
work at the next ranch, so he could stay in shape. He made ten	36
gates. He planted 600 trees. He sheared 950 sheep. The helpers	47
that worked on this ranch said, "He is the fastest worker in the	60
land."	61
Shelly did not get in shape. She said, "I am in shape. My	74
hands are fast. I have never been beaten in a shearing meet."	86
On the day of the meet, Champ sat near the ranch gate. The	99
people from town came up the road. They waved to Champ.	110
The people said, "We made bets that Shelly will beat you."	121
Then they went to the sheep shed and waited.	130
When Shelly came up the road, the people cheered. "Here's	140
Shelly," they yelled.	143
Just before the meet began, Emma Branch came up to	153
Champ. She said, "If you do not beat Shelly, I will not let you	167
stay here. You will have to get your things and leave this ranch."	180
Champ didn't say a thing. He just sat and waited.	190
"We are ready for a shearing meet," a woman yelled. "Let's	201
go."	202

A Note to the Parent

Listen to the student read the passage. Count the number of words read in one minute and the number of errors.

Number of words read _____ Number of errors _____

We read the story _____ times.

(Parent's/Listener's) signature _____

Date _____

Reading fluency

Name _____

Part 1

Read the words in the box. Then fill in the blanks.

eat	slop	run	ran	slabs	see
fish	work	yellow	meat	pick	chomp
fresh	sleeve	meet	sheet	better	score

Chee had met a _____ dog in a _____ plant. The dog was

named Rop, and he _____ the plant. He said that he was _____

than Chee at doing things. Chee got mad. So a _____ was set between Rop

and Chee.

Rop said, "We will begin by seeing how fast we can _____."

Rop told a worker, "Get me 2 _____ of fresh meat."

Part 2

The words in the first column have endings.
Write the same words without endings in the second column.

_____ played

_____ checker

_____ eating

_____ handed

Part 3

Copy the sentences.

She told the best joke.

_____

Chee began to stammer and say odd things.

_____

Vocabulary/context clues, inflectional suffixes, copying sentences

Name _____

Part 4

Chee Meets Rop

Chee worked as a slate stacker for nearly a year. By then,	12
her rate of stacking was very good. But she was getting a little	25
sick of her job. "Stack, stack, stack," she said. "It's time to do	38
something else." So she went to the woman who ran the slate	50
plant and said, "I think I have to quit and get another job."	63
The woman said, "You have been a good worker. Good	73
luck."	74
Chee left the plant and went looking for work. She came to	86
a sleeve plant. They made sleeves for coats in this plant.	97
Chee went into the plant and said to the people working in	109
a big room, "Where is the person who runs this plant?"	120
They went, "Ho, ho. We do not work for a person."	131
Chee told them, "You must work for someone. Show me	141
who."	142
A man stepped up to Chee. The man said, "Step into that	154
room and you will see who runs this plant. His name is Rop."	167
So Chee stepped into the room. Then she stopped. There	177
was no man seated at the desk. There was a yellow dog at the	191
desk.	192
The yellow dog slapped a stamp on a letter.	201

A Note to the Parent

Listen to the student read the passage. Count the number of words read in one minute and the number of errors.

Number of words read _____ Number of errors _____

We read the story _____ times.

(Parent's/Listener's) signature _____

Date _____

Reading fluency

Name _____

Part 1

Cross out the words that don't have **ea.**

rail	mean	hear	main	each	sleep
shear	began	these	tail	smell	beat
seating	real	pail	neck	between	reach

Part 2

Read the words in the box. Then fill in the blanks.

tricking	slapped	lap	sleeves	handed
stammer	making	slabs	slap	store
stabbed	coats	fast	score	wool

Chee and Rop went into the sleeve-_____ room of the plant. There

Rop said, "I will get the best _____ for this meet. We will see how fast that

_____ dog can slap sleeves in _____. The dog that slaps sleeves

fastest will win."

Rop _____ Chee a needle. Chee went very fast, but she _____

herself with the needle.

Part 3

The words in the first column have endings.
Write the same words without endings in the second column.

tricking	
ended	
sleeves	
making	

Sound/symbol correspondence, vocabulary/context clues, inflectional suffixes

Rop and Chee Have a Meet

Chee had met a yellow dog in a sleeve plant. The yellow	12
dog was named Rop, and he ran the plant. He said that he was	26
better than Chee at doing things. Chee got mad. So a meet was	39
set between Rop and Chee. Rop said, "We will see if you can	52
beat me in this meet."	57
Rop yelled to the workers in the sleeve plant. "Stop sleeving	68
and get in here fast," he said. The workers ran into the room.	81
Rop said, "Chee and I are going to have a meet. We will begin	95
by seeing how fast we can eat."	102
Rop told a worker, "Get me 2 slabs of fresh meat. Drop the	115
slabs on the scale and see that they are the same."	126
A woman ran from the plant. She went to the store. She	138
grabbed 2 slabs of meat that were on sale. She got back to the	152
plant and dropped them on the scale. Each slab was the same.	164
Rop handed a slab to Chee. "Here's your slab. See if you can	177
keep up with me." Then he said, "When you hear me say, 'Go,'	190
get your teeth into that meat. Get set . . ."	198
Chee was ready to eat.	203

A Note to the Parent   Listen to the student read the passage. Count the number of words read in one minute and the number of errors.

Number of words read _____   Number of errors _____

We read the story _____ times.

(Parent's/Listener's) signature _____

Date _____

Reading fluency

Name _____

Part 1

The words in the first column have endings.
Write the same words without endings in the second column.

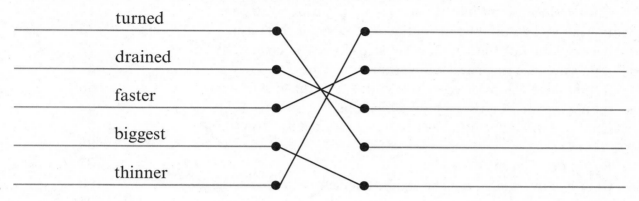

turned

drained

faster

biggest

thinner

Part 2

Write the words.

can   +   not   =   _____

any   +   body   =   _____

my   +   self   =   _____

some   +   one   =   _____

Part 3

Copy the sentences.

He sold gas at the boat ramp.

_____

She did not hear waves on the shore.

_____

Inflectional suffixes, compound words, copying sentences

Part 4

Sleeve Slapping

Chee and Rop went into the sleeve-making room of the	10
plant. There Rop said, "I will get the best score for this meet.	23
We will see how fast that lap dog can slap sleeves on coats. The	37
dog that slaps sleeves fastest will get the best score."	47
Rop handed Chee a needle. Rop said, "Take this needle and	58
get set to go. And don't stab yourself. Ho, ho."	68
Chee was mad. She held the needle and waited for Rop to	80
say, "Go."	82
Rop said, "Get set . . . go."	87
Chee went very fast, but she stabbed herself with the needle.	98
"Ow," she said.	101
"Ho, ho," Rop said, "That lap dog just stabbed herself. Ho,	112
ho, ho, hee, hee." As Rop was ho-heeing, he did not see where	125
his needle was going, and he stabbed himself. "Ow," he said.	136
"Ho, hee, hep, hep, hep," Chee said.	143
Rop yelled, "Stop. This meet is over. I have slapped seven	154
sleeves on coats. So I am the champ, and I get the best score.	168
Let's hear it for me."	173
"Stop," Chee said. "I have slapped seven sleeves on coats,	183
too. So my score is the same as yours."	192
Chee was sore where the needle went into her, but she was	204
glad that Rop had stabbed himself, too.	211

A Note to the Parent Listen to the student read the passage. Count the number of words read in one minute and the number of errors.

Number of words read _____ Number of errors _____

We read the story _____ times.

(Parent's/Listener's) signature _____

Date _____

Reading fluency

Name _____

Part 1
Cross out the words that don't have **ee**.

steered	mean	hear	book	feel	sleep
cheer	began	these	sleeve	smell	beat
seating	wheel	deer	neck	between	steel

Part 2
Write the words.

any + one = _____

some + body = _____

her + self = _____

down + hill = _____

Part 3
Copy the sentences.

The boat was in the middle of the sea.

_____

The goat ate a hole in the boat.

_____

Part 4
The words in the first column have endings.
Write the same words without endings in the second column.

holes

baking

ordered

Sound/symbol correspondence, compound words, copying sentences, inflectional suffixes

Part 5

Sink That Ship

Kit made a boat. She made the boat of tin. The nose of the	14
boat was very thin. Kit said, "I think that this boat is ready for	28
me to take on the lake." So Kit went to the lake with her boat.	43
Her boat was a lot of fun. It went fast. But when she went	57
to dock it at the boat ramp, she did not slow it down. And the	72
thin nose of the boat cut a hole in the boat ramp.	84
The man who sold gas at the boat ramp got mad. He said,	97
"That boat cuts like a blade. Do not take the boat on this lake	111
any more. Take it where you will not run into things."	122
So Kit did not take her boat to the lake any more. She went	136
to the sea with her boat. She said, "There is a lot of room in the	152
sea. I will not run this boat into any docks."	162
So Kit went on the sea with her boat. The nose of her boat	176
went into the waves like a blade. Kit's boat went faster and	188
faster. She said, "I am a good sailor."	196
After a while, she did not see the shore of the sea any more.	210

A Note to the Parent

Listen to the student read the passage. Count the number of words read in one minute and the number of errors.

Number of words read _____ Number of errors _____

We read the story _____ times.

(Parent's/Listener's) signature _____

Date _____

Reading fluency

Part 1

The words in the first column have endings.
Write the same words without endings in the second column.

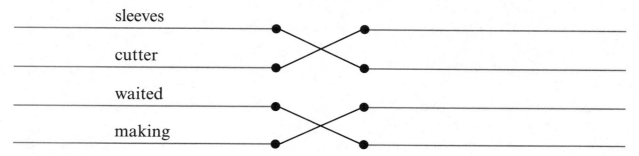

_____ sleeves

_____ cutter

_____ waited

_____ making

Part 2

Cross out the words that don't have **oa**.

goat	mean	boat	book	feel	loading
float	began	these	board	coat	beat

Part 3

Write the words.

an   +   other =   _____

some +   one   =   _____

Part 4

Read the item and fill in the circle next to the answer.
Write the answer in the blank.

1. Kit put rocks in the _____of her boat.

   ○ back   ○ front   ○ top   ○ side

2. Kit said, "Things go fast when they go _____."

   ○ closer   ○ faster   ○ downhill   ○ through

3. The boat made a hole in the _____ of the bank.

   ○ back   ○ front   ○ slide   ○ side

Suffixes, sound/symbol correspondence, compound words, comprehension items

The Goat and Kit's Boat

Kit's boat was in the middle of the sea. It had made a	13
hole in a big ship. The big ship went down. Seventeen men,	25
47 women, three dogs, and a pet goat got in Kit's boat. So Kit	39
made holes in the bottom of the boat to drain the water from	52
the boat.	54
And the water did begin to drain, but not very fast. Kit	66
said, "These holes are not letting water out faster than water is	78
coming in the boat. We need a bigger hole in the bottom."	90
A sailor said, "We left our tools on board the big ship, so we	104
have no way to make bigger holes."	111
A man said, "So let's just yell for help. HELP, HELP."	122
"Hush up," Kit said. "We will get back to shore if we just	135
keep our heads and think of a way to make a big hole that will	150
drain water very fast."	154
An old woman said, "My pet goat likes to eat tin. Maybe he	167
can eat a hole in the bottom of this tin boat."	178
"Yes," Kit said. "Let's see what that goat can do." Then she	190
ordered everybody to make room for the goat to eat.	200

A Note to the Parent

Listen to the student read the passage. Count the number of words read in one minute and the number of errors.

Number of words read _____   Number of errors _____

We read the story _____ times.

(Parent's/Listener's) signature _____

Date _____

Reading fluency

Part 1

Write the words.

good + bye = _____

no + thing = _____

any + body = _____

down + hill = _____

six + teen = _____

Part 2

Read the words in the box. Then fill in the blanks.

sail	boat	nobody	light	aim	white
bike	save	yellow	nothing	green	slow
red	sell	send	steak	pain	float

Kit said, "I am going to _____ this boat and get a _____.

This boat is _____ but a _____."

Then she said to herself, "I can have a lot of fun with a bike. If I get a

_____ bike, it will be very _____, so I'll fly over town."

Part 3

Cross out the words that don't have **ol**.

| goat | told | boat | book | fold | loading |
| float | began | old | cold | meal | bolted |

Compound words, vocabulary/context clues, sound/symbol correspondence

Name _____

Part 4

Kit's Boat Goes Faster and Faster

This is another story about Kit and her tin boat. Kit had	12
her boat at the dock. She was fixing the hole that the goat	25
made in the boat. She painted her boat green. Then she asked	37
the man who sold gas at the dock, "Where can I get some big	51
rocks?"	52
The man said, "Why do you need big rocks?"	61
Kit said, "I will drop them in the front of my boat."	73
The man asked, "Why will you do that?"	81
Kit said, "So that my boat will go faster. I don't like boats	94
that go slow."	97
The man said, "How will the rocks in the front of your boat	110
make the boat go faster?"	115
Kit said, "Don't you see? The rocks will make the front of	127
my boat lower than the back of my boat. So my boat will be	141
going downhill. Things go very fast when they go downhill."	151
The man said, "Ho, ho. Those rocks will just make your	162
boat go slower."	165
But Kit got rocks and dropped them in the front of her	177
boat. Then she said, "Now it is time to see how fast this boat	191
will run."	193
The front of the boat was very low in the water.	204

A Note to the Parent

Listen to the student read the passage. Count the number of words read in one minute and the number of errors.

Number of words read _____   Number of errors _____

We read the story _____ times.

(Parent's/Listener's) signature _____

Date _____

Reading fluency

Name _____

Part 1

Cross out the words that don't have **sh**.

shape	with	chest	shift	what
which	chop	fish	much	cheer

Part 2

The words in the first column have endings.
Write the same words without endings in the second column.

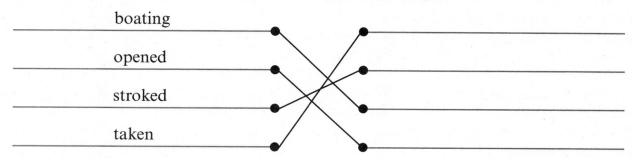

boating

opened

stroked

taken

Part 3

Write the words.

every   +   thing   =   _____

through +   out   =   _____

good   +   bye   =   _____

with   +   out   =   _____

Part 4

Copy the sentences.

The shop man looked at the motor.

_____

She handed three books to him.

_____

Sound/symbol correspondence, inflectional suffixes, compound words, copying sentences

Name _____

Part 5

Kit Makes Her Boat Lighter

Kit was in bad shape. She said, "I can fix things up."	12
The cop said, "Do not try to bribe us. This is a crime."	25
Kit said to her, "I was not trying to bribe you. But you must	39
help me. I need yellow paint."	45
The cop said, "Why do you need yellow paint?"	54
Kit said, "Get me the paint, and you will see."	64
So the cop got another cop to run for the paint. The cop	77
stepped in front of Kit and said, "Do not try to leave." When	90
the other cop came back with the can of yellow paint, Kit	102
smiled.	103
Then she took the lid from the can and began to paint her	116
boat yellow.	118
"What are you doing?" the cops asked. "How can it help	129
anything to paint that boat yellow?"	135
Kit grinned and said, "You will see."	142
Kit got in the boat, and the boat began to float up into	155
the sky. The cops said, "Do you see what I see? That boat is	169
floating in the sky."	173
Kit smiled. Then she hollered down to the cops, "Goodbye."	183
The cops hollered, "Why is that boat floating?"	191
Kit said, "You see, the boat was green, and now it is yellow."	204

A Note to the Parent
Listen to the student read the passage. Count the number of words read in one minute and the number of errors.

Number of words read _____ Number of errors _____

We read the story _____ times.

(Parent's/Listener's) signature _____

Date _____

Reading fluency

Name _____

Part 1
Write the words.

door + way = _____

home + work = _____

no + thing = _____

some + one = _____

Part 2
Cross out the words that don't have **ck.**

cash	packing	clapped	clocks	creek	trucker
rocked	neck	chops	milked	black	thinking

Part 3
Read the words in the box. Then fill in the blanks.

jumped	saw	bolts	tossed	mean	roar
tore	need	smiled	rod	grabbed	worker
fixed	whispered	motor	rubbed	reader	words

Molly said, "Here is the book. It tells where everything is on the _____.

Read the book, and it will tell you what you _____ to know."

So Molly went to the street and _____ into her hot rod. She

_____ the wheel, and she _____ down the street.

Henry took his book and _____ to himself, "I wish I was a better

_____."

Compound words, sound/symbol correspondence, vocabulary/context clues

Part 4

Henry's Hot Rod

Henry had a hot rod. He ran his hot rod very fast down the	14
freeway. But he ran it too fast, and—wham!—there went his	26
cam shaft. Henry said, "Now my hot rod will not go."	37
A truck came and dragged Henry's hot rod back to a motor	49
shop. The shop man looked at the motor. Then he rubbed	60
his chin. He said, "I don't think I can get to this job for three	75
weeks. When do you need this heap?"	82
Henry said, "That hot rod is not a heap. Why can't you get	95
to it now?"	98
The shop man rubbed his chin. Then he said, "I don't have	110
time."	111
The shop man said, "I have three other jobs. When I get	123
them fixed, I can work on your rod."	131
Henry said, "Where can I take my hot rod to get it fixed now?"	145
The shop man said, "There is no shop in town that can do	158
the work now. They have lots of jobs."	166
"Why is that?" Henry asked.	171
"Because people go too fast when they go down the	181
freeway," the shop man said.	186
Henry said, "I will not wait. I will fix my motor at home."	199
"That seems like the best thing to do," the shop man said.	211

A Note to the Parent

Listen to the student read the passage. Count the number of words read in one minute and the number of errors.

Number of words read _____   Number of errors _____

We read the story _____ times.

(Parent's/Listener's) signature _____

Date _____

Reading fluency

Name _____

Part 1

The words in the first column have endings.
Write the same words without endings in the second column.

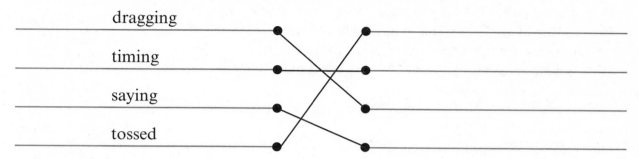

dragging

timing

saying

tossed

Part 2

Write the words.

some + body = _____

up + side = _____

with + out = _____

down + town = _____

Part 3

Read the item and fill in the circle next to the answer.
Write the answer in the blank.

1. Henry was trying to fix a broken cam _____.

   ○ shift   ○ stick   ○ shaft   ○ stack

2. After a while, his motor was in little _____.

   ○ gears   ○ bits   ○ rods   ○ bolts

3. Molly fixed her hot rod because she was able to _____.

   ○ work   ○ know   ○ bolt   ○ read

Inflectional suffixes, compound words, comprehension items

Part 4

Henry's Sister Helps Him

Henry got a book on fixing motors. Henry went home with	11
the book. He sat in his hot rod and looked at the words in the	26
book, but Henry did not know how to read those words.	37
Here is what it said in the book: "There are three bolts that	50
hold this end of the cam shaft."	57
Here is what Henry was reading: "Where are there belts that	68
hold this end for a came shaft."	75
Henry said, "What does that mean?"	81
He kept reading. Here is what it said in his book: "When	93
you take the seals from the shaft, you press on them and then	106
lift them from the shaft."	111
This is what Henry said when he was reading those words:	122
"Why take and steal I dress and then lifted them of the shaft."	135
Henry said, "I don't know what this book means." He	145
tossed the book down and said, "I don't need a book to fix this	159
motor. I have seen people work on motors, and I don't think it	172
will be a very big job."	178
So Henry began to work on his motor. While he was taking	190
some bolts from the motor, a flat strip fell on his foot.	202

A Note to the Parent

Listen to the student read the passage. Count the number of words read in one minute and the number of errors.

Number of words read _____ Number of errors _____

We read the story _____ times.

(Parent's/Listener's) signature _____

Date _____

Reading fluency

Part 1

Write the words.

some + body = _____

up + set = _____

with + out = _____

door + way = _____

Part 2

The words in the first column have endings.
Write the same words without endings in the second column.

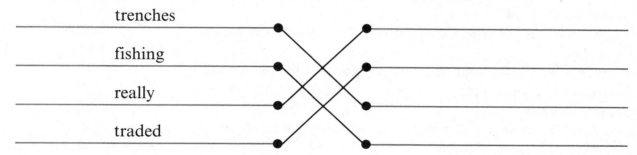

trenches

fishing

really

traded

Part 3

Read the words in the box. Then fill in the blanks.

rested	tires	sell	ripped	site	grip
crime	bikes	rid	roads	gripe	deal
conned	steal	ships	ready	paths	robbed

Kit said, "I think I will get _____ of this boat. It makes

_____ sink. It has _____ up 2 docks. It has

made _____ and trenches. It tore holes in the bank, and that is

a bad _____."

Kit had a lot to _____ over. So she said, "I will _____ the

boat."

Compound words, suffixes, vocabulary/context clues

Part 4

Molly Fixes Her Hot Rod

Henry was trying to fix his motor, but he was not doing very	13
well. He was looking at the words in his book on motors, but	26
Henry did not know what they said. The book said: "To turn a	39
cam shaft, you file each cam."	45
But this is what Henry said as he was reading: "To turn a	58
cam shaft, you fill each cam."	64
Henry said, "What does that mean?" He tossed the book	74
aside and said, "That book is not helping me very much. I can	87
do the job myself." So Henry worked and worked.	96
After a while, his motor was in little bits. Now he did not	109
have a motor. He had a heap of steel.	118
"Where is the cam shaft?" he asked as he looked at the big	131
pile of steel.	134
He picked up a big gear. "Is this a cam shaft?" he asked. He	148
ran his hand over the teeth of the gear. "These things must be	161
the cams," he said.	165
Henry was looking at the gear when a truck came down the	177
street. The truck was dragging his sister's hot rod.	186
Molly was mad. She ran over to Henry and said, "Where is	198
that book?"	200

A Note to the Parent

Listen to the student read the passage. Count the number of words read in one minute and the number of errors.

Number of words read _____   Number of errors _____

We read the story _____ times.

(Parent's/Listener's) signature _____

Date _____

Reading fluency

Lesson 46

Name _____

Part 1
Read the words in the box. Then fill in the blanks.

faster	really	lifted	ready	sold	worker
tires	fastest	robber	diver	zip	float
bikes	traded	back	pile	nose	slower

The con man had _____ his clock, his cash, his ring, and five

_____ with holes in them for Kit's tin boat.

Now the con man was _____ to become the best bank _____

in the west. He said, "I will _____ rocks in the _____ of this

boat. The more rocks I pile, the _____ it will go."

Part 2
Match the words and complete them.

covered	rock
rocket	i
zipped	vered
idea	ped

Part 3
The words in the first column have endings.
Write the same words without endings in the second column.

diver

looked

flying

lifted

Vocabulary/context clues, writing words, suffixes

Part 4

Kit's Trade

Kit said, "I think I will get rid of this boat. It makes ships	14
sink. It has ripped up 2 docks. It has made paths and trenches.	27
It tore holes in the bank, and that is a bad crime."	39
Kit had a lot to gripe over. So she said, "I will sell the boat."	54
She made a note and stuck it on the side of the tin boat. The	69
note said:	71
FOR SALE. A TIN BOAT	76
I WILL TRADE FOR A BIKE.	82
The con man was in town. He had five tires. Each tire had a	96
hole in it.	99
The con man said, "I will sit at this site until I see someone	113
to con." So he sat down on the tires. He was very tired.	126
While he rested, Kit came up the dock. The con man said	138
to himself, "If I can con this woman, I can get rid of my tires.	153
Then I will get some pike to eat. I like fish."	164
The con man said, "I have some fine tires if you have	176
something to trade."	179
Kit said, "I have a boat to trade, but I don't like to trade for	194
tires. I need a bike."	199
The con man said, "Trade your boat for these tires."	209

A Note to the Parent   Listen to the student read the passage. Count the number of words read in one minute and the number of errors.

Number of words read _____   Number of errors _____

We read the story _____ times.

(Parent's/Listener's) signature _____

Date _____

Reading fluency

Name _____

Part 1

Write **1, 2,** or **3** in front of each sentence to show when these things happened in the story. Then write the sentences in the blanks.

_____ The cops and their nine dogs ran up to the con man.

_____ The con man was sticking to the seat of the boat.

_____ The con man said, "This is a space ship, and I come from space."

1. _____

_____

2. _____

_____

3. _____

_____

Part 2

The words in the first column have endings.
Write the same words without endings in the second column.

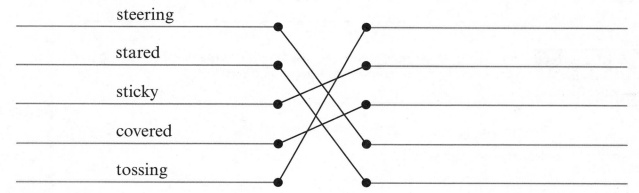

steering

stared

sticky

covered

tossing

Part 3

Copy the sentences.

She is the woman who runs the cotton mill.

_____

Slowly he began to stand up.

_____

Sequence, suffixes, copying sentences

Part 4

The Con Man Gets Cotton Taffy Pike

The con man had traded his clock, his cash, his ring, and	12
five tires with holes in them for Kit's tin boat.	22
Now the con man was ready to become the best bank	33
robber in the West. He said, "I will pile rocks in the nose of this	48
boat. The more rocks I pile, the faster it will go. So I will make	63
this boat the fastest thing there is."	70
So the con man slid the boat into deep water near the dock.	83
Then the con man got a big pile of rocks. He dropped ten rocks	97
into the nose of the boat. Then he dropped ten more.	108
He said, "Now this boat will go very fast." The nose of the	121
boat was low in the water.	127
The con man heaped ten more rocks into the nose of the	139
boat. Then he said, "Now this boat will . . . sink." And it did.	151
The nose of the boat went down. And "glub, blub," the boat	163
went to the bottom of the sea.	170
The con man made a deal with a skin diver. The con man	183
gave the skin diver a coat.	189
The skin diver went under the water and lifted the pile of	201
rocks from the boat.	205

A Note to the Parent — Listen to the student read the passage. Count the number of words read in one minute and the number of errors.

Number of words read _____   Number of errors _____

We read the story _____ times.

(Parent's/Listener's) signature _____

Date _____

Reading fluency

Name _____

Part 1

The words in the first column have endings.
Write the same words without endings in the second column.

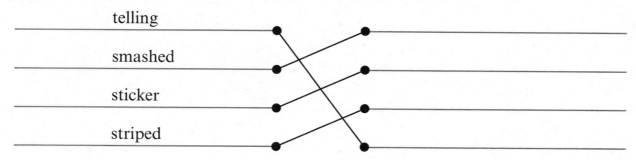

| telling |
| smashed |
| sticker |
| striped |

Part 2

Write the words.

boat   +   load   =   _____

home   +   work   =   _____

through +   out   =   _____

Part 3

Write **1, 2,** or **3** in front of each sentence to show when these things happened in the story. Then write the sentences in the blanks.

_____ The con man began to run with the bags of gold, but he did not run very fast.

_____ The con man took bags of gold from the bank.

_____ The con man said, "I am from space, and I will get you."

1. _____

_____

2. _____

_____

3. _____

_____

Suffixes, compound words, sequence

Name _____

Part 4

A Thing from Space

The con man was zipping here and there in Kit's tin boat.	12
The boat went into a fish-packing plant, into a taffy plant, and	24
into a cotton mill. The con man was a mess. He had a mess of	39
cotton taffy pike in his boat. The steering wheel had taffy on it.	52
The con man said, "I must go somewhere and hide. I must	64
throw the rocks out of this boat so that it will slow down."	77
He began tossing cotton taffy rocks from the nose of the	88
boat. The boat went slower and slower. Then the con man	99
began heaving the pile of pike from the boat. Soon the main	111
street of the town had cotton taffy on it. The boat began to	124
slow down.	126
The con man said, "Now I will run and hide before the cops	139
come here." But when he went to slip from the boat, he said, "I	153
am sticking to the seat. This taffy will not let go of me."	166
The cops and their nine dogs ran up to the con man. The	179
man from the dock ran up to him. The man hollered, "That is	192
the man who smashed my dock into bits."	200

A Note to the Parent

Listen to the student read the passage. Count the number of words read in one minute and the number of errors.

Number of words read _____   Number of errors _____

We read the story _____ times.

(Parent's/Listener's) signature _____

Date _____

Reading fluency

Name _____

Part 1

Write the word **trying.** Make a line over **ing.** _____

Write the word **moaned.** Make a line under **ed.** _____

Part 2

The words in the first column have endings.
Write the same words without endings in the second column.

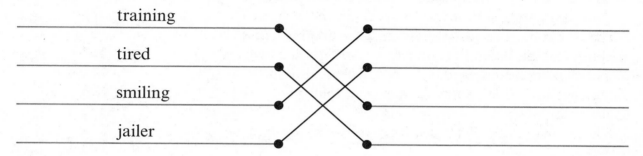

training

tired

smiling

jailer

Part 3

Read the words in the box. Then fill in the blanks.

yelling	three	grain	seven	hair	pike
five	hard	slipped	rain	thing	leg
slapped	griping	drained	steps	trying	nose
raining	tired	light	jumped	drain	like

It was _____ and the con man was _____ about the

_____. He said, "My plan is going down the _____."

He was trying to run with _____ bags of gold, but they were not

_____. He did not run fast. The cotton in his _____ was running

down his _____. He did not see where he was going. He slipped in a pile of

slippery _____ and fell down.

Part 4

Copy the sentence.

They began to lick the taffy. _____

Sound/symbol correspondence, inflectional suffixes, vocabulary/context clues, copying sentences

Lesson 49   **83**

Part 4

The Bank Robbery Fails

The con man made everybody think that he was from space.	11
He was a big mass of cotton lint. The cotton lint was sticking	24
to the taffy. And the taffy was sticking to the con man's skin. It	38
was sticking to everything. The con man said to himself, "I will	50
give these people the scare of their lives."	58
He held up his hands and said a deep "Rrrrr."	68
Three dogs went, "Ooowww," and ran down the street.	77
Then the con man said, "I am from space, and I will get you."	91
The dock man said, "I'm going to run to the sea and dive	104
in." That is what he did. So did the people from the plants.	117
The cops said, "Let's not make this space thing mad." They	128
smiled at him.	131
The con man said, "Rrrrr. I will get you." He began to go	144
for the cops.	147
The cops said, "We had better leave this spot." And they did.	159
They ran down the street and—splash!—they dived into the sea.	171
The con man was standing in the middle of the street.	182
Nobody was near him. He said, "Wow! This is fun. I think I'll	195
go into the bank and see if I can pick up some bags of gold."	210

A Note to the Parent

Listen to the student read the passage. Count the number of words read in one minute and the number of errors.

Number of words read _____ Number of errors _____

We read the story _____ times.

(Parent's/Listener's) signature _____

Date _____

Reading fluency

Part 1

Write the word **digging.** Make a line over **ing.** _____

Write the word **lower.** Make a line under **er.** _____

Part 2

Write **1, 2,** or **3** in front of each sentence to show when these things happened in the story.
Then write the sentences in the blanks.

_____ The other bugs gave the dusty bug a dime to stay in the cool mine.

_____ The bugs went inside a big hole to be in a cool spot.

_____ The mother bug saw the dusty bug digging.

1. _____

_____

2. _____

_____

3. _____

_____

Part 3

The words in the first column have endings.
Write the same words without endings in the second column.

leaves

lower

hotter

walked

Sound/symbol correspondence, sequence, inflectional suffixes

Part 4

The Con Man Gets Busted

It was raining, and the con man was griping about the rain.	12
He said, "My plan is going down the drain."	21
He was trying to run with the three bags of gold, but they	34
were not light, and he did not run fast. The cotton in his hair was	49
running down his nose. He did not see where he was going. He	62
slipped on a pile of slippery pike and—plop, plop, plop!—the	74
con man hit the street, and the three bags of gold landed on the	88
con man.	90
A little boy was standing near the con man. The boy said,	102
"You are not from space. I can see that you are just a wet man."	117
The lint was sliding from the con man's hair, from his hands,	129
from his nose, and from his coat. The rain was coming down	141
very fast, and the con man was very, very wet.	151
A dog ran up to the con man and began to lick the taffy	165
from his hand. "Don't bite me," the con man said. And the dog	178
did not bite. It licked and licked. It liked the taffy. Then three	191
cats came up to the con man. They began to lick the taffy.	204

A Note to the Parent — Listen to the student read the passage. Count the number of words read in one minute and the number of errors.

Number of words read _____ Number of errors _____

We read the story _____ times.

(Parent's/Listener's) signature _____

Date _____

Reading fluency

Part 1

Read the item and fill in the circle next to the answer.
Write the answer in the blank.

1. The dusty bug liked _____.
   ○ bills   ○ shovels   ○ dills   ○ smells

2. The bug said, "I don't have _____ with me."
   ○ pickles   ○ cash   ○ tubs   ○ mine

3. The bug dug into the _____ and got a big pickle.
   ○ store   ○ bag   ○ mine   ○ tub

Part 2

Write the word **outside**. Make a line over **out**. _____

Write the word **another**. Make a line under **er**. _____

Part 3
Match the words and complete them.

joking		gri
rotten		cl
clerk		king
grinned		ten

Part 4
Copy the sentence.
The dusty bug smiled from the door of the store.

_____

Comprehension items, sound/symbol correspondence, writing words, copying sentence

Name _____

Part 5

The Bug That Dug

There was a bug. That bug liked to dig. He dug and dug.	13
His mother said, "Why do you keep digging? The rest of us	25
bugs eat leaves and sit in the shade. But you dig and dig."	38
"When I dig, I feel happy," the digging bug said. "I like to	51
make holes."	53
So he made holes. When he stopped digging, he was dusty.	64
His brothers and sisters said, "You are a mess. You have dust	76
on your back. What are you doing?"	83
The bug said, "When I dig, I feel happy." And so that bug	96
dug and dug.	99
Then something happened. The days began to get hotter	108
and hotter. The sun was so hot that the other bugs said, "We	121
cannot stay here. It is too hot. We must go to a spot that is not	137
so hot."	139
They walked here and there, but they did not find a spot	151
that felt cool. Then they came to a big hole in the side of a hill.	167
They said, "Let's go down this hole. It looks cool inside."	178
The bugs went inside the hole. Then the mother bug	188
stopped. She said, "Did you hear that? I hear something in this	200
hole."	201

A Note to the Parent

Listen to the student read the passage. Count the number of words read in one minute and the number of errors.

Number of words read _____   Number of errors _____

We read the story _____ times.

(Parent's/Listener's) signature _____

Date _____

Reading fluency

Name _____

Part 1

Match the words and complete them.

orange ————●   ●———— man

holding ————●   ●———— hold

drink ————●   ●———— or

woman ————●   ●———— dr

Part 2

Read the words in the box. Then fill in the blanks.

table	grabbed	stopped	bib	fixed	binging
taken	broken	dropped	cheer	deer	door
dropping	floor	fixing	making	sound	leak

The clock maker _____ the clock and _____ it. The

clock made a loud _____ when it hit the _____. The

_____ fell out. A spring went, "bop." The clock went, "bing, bing, ding."

The clock maker said, "That clock is _____. Let me make a bid on

_____ it."

Part 3

Write the words.

ding + ing = _____

real + ly = _____

sleep + ing = _____

loud + ly = _____

Writing words, vocabulary/context clues, suffixes

Part 4

The Bug and the Pickle Tub

The dusty bug was resting in his mine. It was hot outside.	12
He had a rusty shovel. He had been digging with the shovel, but	25
now he was tired. He said, "I need to eat. I like dill pickles, but	40
I don't have any dills."	45
He tossed the shovel to one side. Then he came out of his	58
mine. The sun was very hot. The bug went to a store. Then he	72
picked up a tub of pickles. He said to the clerk, "Will you bill	86
me for these dill pickles?"	91
The clerk said, "No, we do not bill for pickles. You must	103
pay cash in this store."	108
The bug said, "I don't have cash with me. But if you send	121
me a bill, I will pay for it."	129
The clerk said, "You did not hear me. I said that we do not	143
bill for dill pickles."	147
The bug said, "That's fine with me. Now that I smell these	159
pickles, I can tell that they are rotten."	167
"They are not rotten," the clerk said. "They are the best	178
pickles in town."	181
The bug began to laugh. Then he said, "These pickles are so	193
bad that they will make you sick if you eat them."	204

A Note to the Parent

Listen to the student read the passage. Count the number of words read in one minute and the number of errors.

Number of words read _____ Number of errors _____

We read the story _____ times.

(Parent's/Listener's) signature _____

Date _____

Reading fluency

Name _____

Part 1

Write **1, 2,** or **3** in front of each sentence to show when these things happened in the story. Then write the sentences in the blanks.

_____ The clock maker slapped a bell into the deer clock.

_____ The clock maker painted the deer yellow.

_____ The woman tossed the clock down, and it broke into parts.

1. _____

_____

2. _____

_____

3. _____

_____

Part 2

The words in the first column have endings.
Write the same words without endings in the second column.

slapped

looked

working

parts

Part 3

Write the word **himself.** Make a line over **self.** _____

Write the word **dabbed.** Make a line under **ed.** _____

Part 4

Copy the sentence.

A woman was standing near the door. _____

Sequence, inflectional suffixes, sound/symbol correspondence

Part 5

The Old Clock Maker

The old clock maker liked to work with plants when he	11
wasn't working with clocks. He had lots of plants in back of	23
his home. Every day after work, he dressed in a bib and went to	37
dabble with his plants. While he dabbled, he talked. He didn't	48
hear himself, so he didn't know that he was saying things very	60
loudly. When he came to a plant that did not have buds, he said,	74
"This plant is a dud because it doesn't have one bud."	85
One day, he was dabbling and talking when his wife came	96
out. She said, "A woman is here. Can you make a bid on fixing	110
a clock?"	112
The old clock maker did not hear her. The clock maker said,	124
"I do not have a rip in my bib."	133
His wife said, "I did not say 'bib,' I said 'bid.' A woman	146
needs a bid. Can you tell her how much she will have to pay?"	160
"I'm not going to the bay," the clock maker said. "I'm going	172
to stay here with the bees and my plants."	181
"Come with me," his wife said. "I will let you speak to the	194
woman." So she led the old clock maker inside.	203

A Note to the Parent

Listen to the student read the passage. Count the number of words read in one minute and the number of errors.

Number of words read _____   Number of errors _____

We read the story _____ times.

(Parent's/Listener's) signature _____

Date _____

Reading fluency

Part 1
Write the words.

every + thing = _____

with + out = _____

door + way = _____

out + side = _____

Part 2
Write **1, 2,** or **3** in front of each sentence to show when these things happened in the story. Then write the sentences in the blanks.

_____ The old clock maker took the clock back to the woman.

_____ An alligator ran across the front of the clock and bit the clock maker's finger.

_____ The clock maker stuck antlers on the alligator and slapped it into the deer clock.

1. _____

_____

2. _____

_____

3. _____

_____

Part 3
The words in the first column have endings.
Write the same words without endings in the second column.

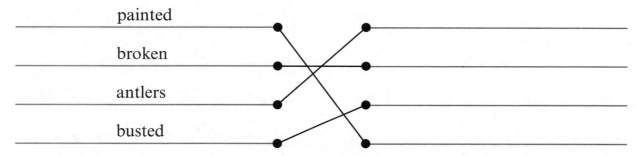

painted

broken

antlers

busted

Compound words, sequence, inflectional suffixes

Part 4

The Deer That Bobbed Like a Frog

The clock maker gave a bid on the clock that he had	12
dropped. He made a bid of eleven dollars. Then he took the	24
clock to his work room. In that room he had lots of clocks.	37
Every hour, the clocks went, "dong, dong," and, "ding, ding."	47
But the clock maker did not hear them.	55
In the work room, the clock maker had a bin of parts from	68
other clocks. He also had a lot of tools for fixing clocks.	80
The clock maker held the clock with the deer. He said, "I	92
will have to paint this clock." So he got a brush and dabbed	105
paint on the clock.	109
He made the clock orange. Then he dabbed paint on the	120
deer. He made the deer yellow.	126
Then he went to his bin of old clocks to look for one that	140
had a good deer. He looked and looked. Then he began to talk	153
to himself. He said, "This is bad. I made a bid on fixing this	167
clock, but I cannot see another clock with a working deer. The	179
best I can see is a clock with a working frog. That frog comes	193
out every hour and bobs up and down."	201

A Note to the Parent

Listen to the student read the passage. Count the number of words read in one minute and the number of errors.

Number of words read _____ Number of errors _____

We read the story _____ times.

(Parent's/Listener's) signature _____

Date _____

Reading fluency

Part 1

Copy the sentences.

The woman tossed the clock into a tree.

_____

A little yellow bird sat on the alligator's antlers.

_____

Part 2

The words in the first column have endings.
Write the same words without endings in the second column.

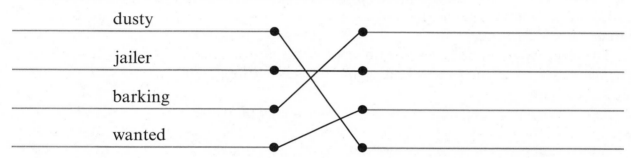

dusty

jailer

barking

wanted

Part 3

Read the words in the box. Then fill in the blanks.

third	home	first	next	stayed	way
leaves	time	came	come	bees	house
pay	play	buy	days	birds	trees

The woman said, "For some _____, I've wanted to get those

_____ into my tree, but this is the _____ time they've

_____ to the tree. Thank you. How can I _____ you?"

"Hand me eleven dollars, and I'll be on my _____ this day," the

clock maker said. So the woman gave the clock maker eleven dollars, and he went

_____.

Copying sentences, suffixes, vocabulary/context clues

Part 4

An Alligator Clock

The clock maker had painted a clock orange. He had made	11
the deer yellow. He had fixed the deer so that it bobbed up and	25
down like a frog. When the clock maker took the clock to the	38
woman, the woman got very mad. She tossed the clock down.	49
The clock maker took the broken clock back to his shop. He	61
was going to fix it again.	67
He had just put his work bib on when his wife came in. She	81
said, "Did you just come in?"	87
"Yes," the clock maker said, "I can grin." And he did.	98
His wife shook her head. Then she said, "A little girl is	110
outside. She wants to know if she can pick weeds in your	122
garden."	123
The clock maker said, "There are no seeds in my garden.	134
The plants are just getting buds. They won't have seeds before	145
the end of summer."	149
"Not seeds," his wife said. "Weeds. The girl wants to pick	160
weeds."	161
"Why does she want to lick weeds?" the clock maker asked.	172
His wife was getting mad. She said, "I will tell her that	184
she can pick weeds. If she does a good job, I will pay her ten	199
dollars."	200

A Note to the Parent

Listen to the student read the passage. Count the number of words read in one minute and the number of errors.

Number of words read _____ Number of errors _____

We read the story _____ times.

(Parent's/Listener's) signature _____

Date _____

Reading fluency

Name _____

Part 1

Write **1**, **2**, or **3** in front of each sentence to show when these things happened in the story. Then write the sentences in the blanks.

_____ The doctor said, "Lock this man up."

_____ The bus took the con man to the rest home.

_____ The con man got down on the floor and growled at the nurse.

1. _____

_____

2. _____

_____

3. _____

_____

Part 2

The words in the first column have endings.
Write the same words without endings in the second column.

_____ taking _____

_____ growled _____

_____ snapping _____

Part 3

Match the words and complete them.

_____ pretty ●   ● dow _____

_____ window ●   ● gar _____

_____ garden ●   ● pre _____

Sequence, inflectional suffixes, writing words

Name _____

Part 4

The Clock in the Tree

The clock maker had taken an alligator from a dusty old	11
clock and had slapped it into the deer clock. The alligator was	23
yellow, and it had antlers. The old man said, "This clock looks	35
just like it did before."	40
So the clock maker took the clock to the woman. The clock	52
maker rapped on her door. The woman came to the door.	63
"What do you want?" she said.	69
"Here it is," the clock maker said. He held up the alligator	81
clock. "This clock is fixed up as good as ever."	91
The woman looked at the clock and said, "Oh, no. I don't	103
want to buy dusty clocks with beads on them. I had a good	116
clock, and you busted that clock. Now you are selling old junk	128
clocks."	129
"Yes," the old clock maker said. "It looks just as good as	141
ever. Here, hold it while I set the hands."	150
Before the woman was able to back away, the clock maker	161
handed her the clock and began to set the hands. As soon as the	175
hands were set for five o'clock, the clock made a loud sound.	187
"Blip, blop," sounded the bell.	192
And here came the alligator. It bobbed up and down.	202

A Note to the Parent Listen to the student read the passage. Count the number of words read in one minute and the number of errors.

Number of words read _____ Number of errors _____

We read the story _____ times.

(Parent's/Listener's) signature _____

Date _____

Reading fluency

Name _____

Part 1
Write the words.

be   +   fore   =   _____

some   +   where   =   _____

any   +   one   =   _____

your   +   self   =   _____

out   +   side   =   _____

Part 2
Copy the sentences.

He tried to get out the window.

_____

They looked around and didn't see anybody.

_____

The doctor took notes on a pad.

_____

Part 3
Write the name of the person each sentence tells about.

     president   **con man**

1. This person had to be a private in the army.   _____

2. This person said, "You must do everything I say."   _____

3. This person marched and marched and marched.   _____

Compound words, copying sentences, characterization

Part 4

The Con Man Acts Like a Dog

When we left the con man, he was in the hospital. He had	13
told the cops and the jailer that he was sick. He really wasn't	26
sick. He was just playing sick. But the cop took him to the	39
hospital. The cop went up to a nurse and said, "Nurse, I have a	53
sick man. He needs help."	58
The nurse said, "We will fix him up fast." She had the con	71
man sit on a cart. Then she took the con man to a room.	85
As soon as she left the room, the con man darted for the	98
door. He peeked outside. But the cop was standing near the	109
door. "Nuts," the con man said. "I will try the window."	120
He darted to the window. He grabbed the handles and	130
opened it wide. Then he looked out. There were bars on the	142
window. "Nuts," the con man said.	148
He sat on the bed and said to himself, "I must think of a	162
trick that will get me out of here." Suddenly he jumped up.	174
"I've got it," he yelled. Then he began to bark like a dog. He	188
had a plan.	191
The nurse came running in. "What's that barking?" she	200
asked.	201

A Note to the Parent — Listen to the student read the passage. Count the number of words read in one minute and the number of errors.

Number of words read _____   Number of errors _____

We read the story _____ times.

(Parent's/Listener's) signature _____

Date _____

Reading fluency

Name _____

Part 1

Write the word **wheat.** Make a line over **ea.** _____

Write the word **hiding.** Make a line under **ing.** _____

Part 2

The words in the first column have endings.
Write the same words without endings in the second column.

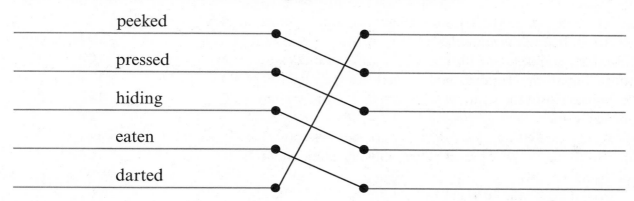

peeked	
pressed	
hiding	
eaten	
darted	

Part 3

Write **1, 2,** or **3** in front of each sentence to show when these things happened in the story. Then write the sentences in the blanks.

_____ The president began to scream, "Oh, my foot. It is stuck in the gate."

_____ The con man and the president hid under the bed.

_____ The man who ran the gate pressed the button, and the gate opened.

1. _____

_____

2. _____

_____

3. _____

_____

Writing words, inflectional suffixes, sequence

Name _____

Part 4

The Con Man Meets the President

The con man had told the doctor that he was very foxy. The	13
doctor had two helpers lock up the con man. The doctor said,	25
"That man thinks he's a fox now."	32
So the helpers took the con man to a little room at the far	46
end of the yard. They said, "You will like this room. You will	59
have a good time."	63
The con man said, "I am too smart for you. I will get out of	78
this room before the sun sets."	84
But the sun set, and the con man hadn't found a way to get	98
out of the room. He pounded on the floor. He tried to get out	112
the window. But the window had bars on it. And the bars did	125
not bend.	127
At last, the con man sat down on the bed. He said, "I will	141
have to think with my brains. There must be some way to get	154
out of here."	157
Somebody said, "It is easy to get out of here."	167
The con man looked around the room, but he did not	178
see anybody. The con man said, "Maybe I am out of it. I am	192
hearing people talk."	195
Just then the con man saw a foot under the bed.	206

A Note to the Parent   Listen to the student read the passage. Count the number of words read in one minute and the number of errors.

Number of words read _____   Number of errors _____

We read the story _____ times.

(Parent's/Listener's) signature _____

Date _____

Reading fluency

Name _____

Part 1

Write the words.

near + by = _____

with + out = _____

be + cause = _____

loud + ly = _____

Part 2

Write **1, 2,** or **3** in front of each sentence to show when these things happened in the story. Then write the sentences in the blanks.

_____ The president said very loudly, "We are from the bug company."

_____ The woman in the main office said, "Take the green car in front of the office."

_____ The con man and the president dressed in white jackets and left the shack.

1. _____

_____

2. _____

_____

3. _____

_____

Part 3

The words in the first column have endings.
Write the same words without endings in the second column.

steered

nearest

stared

Compound words, sequence, inflectional suffixes

Name _____

Part 4

A Foxy Escape—Part 1

The con man was in a room with a man who said that he	14
was President Washington. President Washington said that he	22
was in charge of their escape. The con man was just a private in	36
his army.	38
The next day, the president said, "Soon they will come	48
around to feed us. When we hear them at the door, we will	61
zip under the bed. And we will wait without making a sound.	73
Remember to do everything I say, because I don't want	83
anything to mar my plans."	88
"Yes, sir," the con man said. He was very tired. He had	100
marched and marched. He had taken lots of orders from the	111
president.	112
Just then, there was a sound outside the door. "Quick," the	123
president said. "Dart under the bed. And don't let your feet show."	135
The con man darted under the bed. The president darted	145
under the bed. Then the president whispered, "There is dust	155
under this bed, and dust makes me sneeze."	163
The con man whispered, "Don't sneeze."	169
"Hush up, private," whispered the president.	175
The door opened. The con man peeked out and saw two	186
legs walking across the room. Then he saw two more. "Where	197
are they?" a man asked.	202

A Note to the Parent

Listen to the student read the passage. Count the number of words read in one minute and the number of errors.

Number of words read _____   Number of errors _____

We read the story _____ times.

(Parent's/Listener's) signature _____

Date _____

Reading fluency

Part 1

Cross out the words that don't have **ar**.

chair	alarm	about	drain	started	talking
army	scream	darted	charge	track	sharp

Part 2

Write the name of the person each sentence tells about.

 president   con man

1. This person said, "I need something to eat." _____

2. This person ordered a big lunch for two. _____

3. This person said, "I must get away from this guy." _____

4. This person rolled right off the side of the bed. _____

5. This person said, "Just charge it to the room." _____

6. This person smiled and said, "Tee, hee." _____

Part 3

The words in the first column have endings.
Write the same words without endings in the second column.

_____ suddenly

_____ rapped

_____ snoring

_____ shaved

Sound/symbol correspondence, characterization, suffixes

Part 4

A Foxy Escape—Part 2

The con man ran from the grove of trees. He jogged up to	13
the president. The president smiled and said, "You see, private,	23
the gate is open. And we are free. Let's run down that road	36
before these yokels come after us."	42
So the con man and the president ran down the road. The	54
people from the rest home ran up to the gate. They said to the	68
gate man, "Did you open the gate and let those men escape?"	80
"Yes, I did," the gate man said. "But the first man had his	93
foot stuck in the gate. He was in pain."	102
"You yokel," the people said. Six people began to run after	113
the con man and the president.	119
"I'm getting tired," the con man said. "Let's stop and rest."	130
"Hush up, private," the president said. "You'll never become	139
a major thinking the way you do."	146
"I don't want to become a major," the con man said. "I just	159
want to get out of here."	165
"Then do what I say," the president shouted. "We're going	175
back to the rest home. Follow me."	182
"What?" the con man asked. "We can't go back. They'll get us."	194
"No, no," the president said. "They don't think that we will	205
go back."	207

A Note to the Parent

Listen to the student read the passage. Count the number of words read in one minute and the number of errors.

Number of words read _____ Number of errors _____

We read the story _____ times.

(Parent's/Listener's) signature _____

Date _____

Reading fluency

Name _____

Part 1

Write the word **hamburger.** Make a line over **er.** _____

Write the word **please.** Make a line under **ea.** _____

Part 2

Write **1, 2,** or **3** in front of each sentence to show when these things happened in the story. Then write the sentences in the blanks.

_____ The president said to the man behind the desk, "Give me my money back."

_____ The president cut some hair from the man's wig and made a beard with it.

_____ The president and the con man got into a cab and drove away.

1. _____

_____

2. _____

_____

3. _____

_____

Part 3

Write the name of the person each sentence tells about.

   president   con man   man at the desk

1. This person began to tell a story about a battle.   _____

2. This person said, "We must escape."   _____

3. This person said, "Well, let's dash, buster."   _____

4. This person said that there were bugs in the hotel.   _____

5. This person handed over two hundred dollars.   _____

Sound/symbol correspondence, sequence, characterization

Name _____

Part 4

The Con Man Becomes a Bride

The president and the con man were in the bridal rooms of	12
the big hotel. The president had told the man at the desk that	25
he and the con man were from the bug company. The president	37
had said that somebody called about the bugs in the bridal	48
rooms.	49

The president said, "This is the life." He sat down on the   61
bed. "I need something to eat, private. Go down to the dining   73
room and get a big lunch for us. Charge it to the room."   86

The con man said, "But I'm not—"   93

"Hush up, private," the president yelled. "If you want to   103
stay in this army, you must remember that I am in charge."   115

"Yes, sir," the con man said.   121

The con man went down to the dining room and ordered a   133
big lunch for two. "Charge it to the bridal rooms," he said.   145

Then he went back to the bridal rooms. The president was   156
sleeping on the bed. The con man said to himself, "I must get   169
away from this guy, but I need a plan."   178

He sat in a chair and began to think. The president was in   191
the bed, snoring and snoring. Then the con man jumped up.   202

A Note to the Parent

Listen to the student read the passage. Count the number of words read in one minute and the number of errors.

Number of words read _____   Number of errors _____

We read the story _____ times.

(Parent's/Listener's) signature _____

Date _____

Reading fluency

Name _____

Part 1

The words in the first column have endings.
Write the same words without endings in the second column.

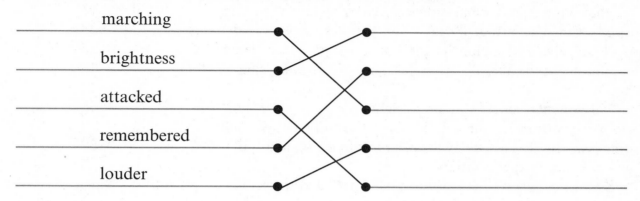

marching

brightness

attacked

remembered

louder

Part 2

Read the item and fill in the circle next to the answer.
Write the answer in the blank.

1. Jean was on night _____ in this story.

   ○ planet   ○ play   ○ march   ○ patrol

2. There were _____ moons in the night sky.

   ○ three   ○ five   ○ third   ○ six

3. The drams moved like a big _____ when they came out of the lake.

   ○ army   ○ patrol   ○ grasshopper   ○ wake

4. The drams would _____ everything in their path.

   ○ stop   ○ eat   ○ reach   ○ wake

Part 3

Write the words.

grass   +   hopper   =   _____

spot   +   light   =   _____

some   +   thing   =   _____

Suffixes, comprehension items, compound words

Part 4

The Escape from the Hotel

The con man and the president were having lunch in the	11
bridal room. The president said, "This room is a mess. I told	23
that bum private to get lunch. But look at the junk he ordered.	36
Hamburgers and cake. The army just isn't what it was years	47
ago."	48
The con man said, "You are so right."	56
"Yes, my dear. Let me tell you about the battle that we had	69
some years back. The enemy army had us holed up in a spot	82
named Valley Forge. We were—"	87
Suddenly, the president stopped. He jumped up and sniffed	96
the air. "I smell the enemy," he said. "They are going to attack.	109
I know it. And I don't even have my army with me. Where is	123
that private?"	125
The president ran to the window and looked down at the	136
street. "There are cop cars down there. We must escape."	146
The president ran to the closet and came back with dress	157
pants and a striped coat. He slipped into them. Then he cut	169
some hair from the con man's wig and made a beard with it. He	183
stuck the beard on his chin. Then he grabbed a top hat from the	197
closet.	198
He looked at the con man and winked.	206

A Note to the Parent

Listen to the student read the passage. Count the number of words read in one minute and the number of errors.

Number of words read _____   Number of errors _____

We read the story _____ times.

(Parent's/Listener's) signature _____

Date _____

Reading fluency

Name _____

Part 1
Write the words.

her + self = _____

what + ever = _____

moon + light = _____

some + body = _____

Part 2
Read the words in the box. Then fill in the blanks.

reached	far	shirt	closer	pressed	springs
skipped	inches	drams	pocket	melted	stabbed
eaten	barracks	messed	light	signaler	stared

Jean couldn't seem to move. She _____ at the drams as they came

_____. They were only about twenty feet from her now.

"Move," she said to herself. But her legs felt as if they had _____.

Then Jean began to think. She _____ for her _____. She

_____ the button. Lights began to flash in the _____. Women

began to yell, "The drams! The drams! Let's get out of here."

And Jean began to run. Now her legs felt like _____. Did she ever run!

Part 3
Copy the sentence.
Suddenly, a sound came from the other room.

_____

Compound words, vocabulary/context clues, copying sentences

Part 4

Jean on Patrol

The night was cool. Jean looked up at the five moons in the	13
night sky. "I will never feel at home on this planet," she said to	27
herself. She was on night patrol. Her job was to patrol a strip	40
that led from the beach of the red lake to the barracks. Nobody	53
liked night patrol, not with the drams.	60
The drams were little animals that came from the red lake.	71
They looked like grasshoppers, but they were bigger. About	80
three times a year, they came out of the lake. When they did,	93
things got very bad. They ate everything in their path. They ate	105
wood and bricks. They ate the yellow plants that lived on the	117
planet.	118
Last year, they had eaten the barracks. Seven years before	128
that, they had attacked some of the women who didn't get out	140
of the barracks. Nobody could find a way to stop them. The	152
drams moved like a big army, with millions and millions of	163
drams marching and eating, marching and eating.	170
Jean had been on the planet for a little more than six	182
months. She had seen the drams before. One night, they had	193
come from the lake making that "bzzzzzz" that they make.	203

A Note to the Parent
Listen to the student read the passage. Count the number of words read in one minute and the number of errors.

Number of words read _____   Number of errors _____

We read the story _____ times.

(Parent's/Listener's) signature _____

Date _____

Reading fluency

Part 1
The words in the first column have endings.
Write the same words without endings in the second column.

_____ streaming

_____ wiggled

_____ trying

_____ eaten

_____ cliffs

Part 2
Write **1, 2,** or **3** in front of each sentence to show when these things happened in the story.

_____ Two women held Jean while the others slapped the drams.

_____ There was a mass of drams on Jean.

_____ Jean found out that Carla was on patrol.

Part 3
Write the name of the person each sentence tells about.

     Jean   Carla   major

1. This person was not in her room.   _____

2. This person made a loud sound with the trumpet.   _____

3. This person wiggled and tried to shake off the drams.   _____

4. This person fell into a hole in the floor of the barracks. _____

5. This person was on patrol near the cliffs.   _____

6. This person said, "You did a brave thing."   _____

Inflectional suffixes, sequence, characterization

Name _____

Part 4

The Drams Attack

For a moment, Jean was frozen as she looked at the	11
drams coming from the lake. She could see them clearly in the	23
moonlight. They were shiny as they moved up the beach.	33
For a moment, Jean didn't remember that she was to signal	44
the barracks as soon as she spotted drams. She wanted to	55
run—run as fast as she could go. She wanted to run as far from	70
the drams as she could get. But she couldn't seem to move. She	83
stared at the drams as they came closer and closer. They were	95
only twenty feet from her now.	101
"Move. Get out of here," she said to herself. But her legs felt	114
as if they had melted.	119
Then Jean began to think. She reached for her signaler.	129
She pressed the button. Lights began to flash in the barracks.	140
Women began to yell, "The drams! The drams! Let's get out of	152
here."	153
And Jean began to run. Now her legs felt like springs. Did	165
she ever run! It was about three blocks from the beach to the	178
barracks, and Jean ran to the barracks so fast that she felt as if	192
she had run only twenty feet.	198
When she got to the barracks, she ran up to the major.	210

A Note to the Parent

Listen to the student read the passage. Count the number of words read in one minute and the number of errors.

Number of words read _____   Number of errors _____

We read the story _____ times.

(Parent's/Listener's) signature _____

Date _____

Reading fluency

Name _____

Part 1

Write **1, 2,** or **3** in front of each sentence to show when these things happened in the story.

_____ Jean tried to think of everything that happened just before the drams went to sleep.

_____ The major told the others why the trumpet made the drams sleep.

_____ Jean gave a blast on Carla's trumpet.

Part 2

The words in the first column have endings.
Write the same words without endings in the second column.

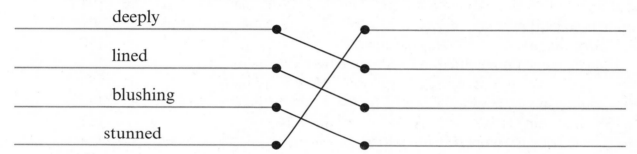

deeply

lined

blushing

stunned

Part 3

Read the words in the box. Then fill in the blanks.

barracks	bubbles	blushed	sound	fill	smiled
animals	horns	hunger	felt	showed	leave
line	march	patrol	water	hungry	blast

One of the women said, "Does that mean that we can stop the drams just by blowing

_____ when they come out of the _____?"

"We can do better than that," the major said. "We can pipe _____ into

the lake. We can keep them from getting _____ for sound. Then they won't

_____ the lake."

The women _____ and looked at each other. Jean was thinking, "Now

night _____ won't be so bad."

Sequence, suffixes, vocabulary/context clues

Name _____

Part 4

Trapped in the Barracks

The drams were at the other end of the barracks. They had	12
eaten the wall, and now they were streaming over the floor.	23
Jean was standing outside the door to Carla's room. Carla was	34
not in sight. Jean had to get out of the barracks before the	47
drams reached her. And she had to find Carla. The drams were	59
coming closer. The "bzzzzzz" was very loud.	66
Jean ran into Carla's room. She grabbed the trumpet from	76
Carla's table. "I can make a loud sound with this horn," Jean	88
said to herself. She took in a lot of air. Then she pressed the	102
trumpet to her lips.	106
"Brrrrroooooooooooo," went the horn.	110
Suddenly the floor shifted. A crash came from the middle of	121
the barracks. The drams were getting closer. "No time to blow	132
the horn again," Jean said to herself. "I must get out of here."	145
She ran from Carla's room. A mass of drams was on the	157
floor. Jean tried to run past them, but one dram got on her leg.	171
It bit a hole in her pants. Jean tried to slap it off, and she tried	187
to run at the same time. Another dram was on her back.	199
"Ow," Jean yelled.	202

A Note to the Parent

Listen to the student read the passage. Count the number of words read in one minute and the number of errors.

Number of words read _____ Number of errors _____

We read the story _____ times.

(Parent's/Listener's) signature _____

Date _____

Reading fluency

Answer Key

Lesson 1

Name _____

Part 1
Match the words.

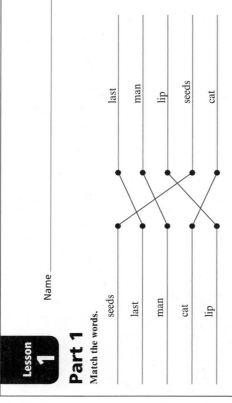

seeds — last
last — man
man — lip
cat — seeds
lip — cat

Part 2

⑤ o e(s)p l m n a a w e r(s)p k u b(s)w q a z d r t y u n b g t y u p l n a z d(s)e(s)

④ (clap)t a o q a s(clap)m f f r t y u p l l a(clap)q e r t s v b l a t(clap)d o x e(clap)s

Part 3
Copy the sentences.

Keep a plant in that sack.

Keep a plant in that sack.

Can the cat sleep in a lap?

Can the cat sleep in a lap?

Fill this pan with sticks.

Fill this pan with sticks.

Directions, part 2: Ask the student, "What sound will you circle in the first row?" (sss) "What word will you circle in the second row?" (clap)

Lesson 1   1

Lesson 2

Name _____

Part 1
Match the words.

lamp — sleep
feeds — stick
sleep — clap
stick — lamp
clap — feeds

Part 2

⑦ e l j a(i)a t r f(i)s d e(i)r c b p(i)t e a g h h n m a(i)o m n b g r e(i)l(i)d e

④ (sit)s e l f i t(sit)s i t h a t(sit)n f i t s i s(sit)i s e t s i f e f i g m i s s a t i s(sit)i f

③ (this)h i t t h e h i m i n(this)t i s t e e t h i f(this)h a t p i t d i d(this)j i n i s

Part 3
Copy the sentences.

Dad can see the cats sleep.

Dad can see the cats sleep.

Plant this seed in the sand.

Plant this seed in the sand.

Did that tack stick the cat?

Did that tack stick the cat?

This ant sits in a back pack.

This ant sits in a back pack.

Directions, part 2: Ask the student, "What sound will you circle in the first row?" (iii) "What word will you circle in the second row?" (sit) "What word will you circle in the third row?" (this)

2   Lesson 2

Name _____

Part 1
Copy the sentences.

This cap fits in that pack.

This cap fits in that pack.

We had no plan for a trip.

We had no plan for a trip.

That truck can go so fast.

That truck can go so fast.

Part 2
Read the sentences in the box.

1. At last she has a black cat.
2. Will that truck slip in mud?
3. Slip this stick in the pack.

Write the first word of these sentences.

2nd sentence _____ *Will*

1st sentence _____ *At*

3rd sentence _____ *Slip*

Part 3
Match the words.

math — cash
hill — teeth
cash — math
truck — hill
teeth — truck

Name _____

Part 1

sh   d e f a c l p o e (sh) s e a (sh) m n j s a (sh) e i p l t h n z s l (sh) f d (sh) f e c r q w ⑤

(flag)   d w (flag) e r o p l e g c z d a (flag) h e r c l a m c l p e (flag) s a t e f l a t v b s p ③

Part 2
Copy the sentences.

Will that milk last us for a week?

Will that milk last us for a week?

I need a pack for the trip.

I need a pack for the trip.

Three deer sleep with the sheep.

Three deer sleep with the sheep.

Part 3
Match the words and complete them.

truck — sh*eep*
sheep — mi*l*k
milk — *p*lant
drink — *dr*ink
plant — tru*ck*

Lesson 5

Name _____

Part 1
Match the words and complete them.

stop
flag
drink
truck
store

dr ink
st ore
fl ag
st op
tr uck

Part 2
Copy the sentences.

We will go for more fish at the store.

We will go for more fish at the store.

She sat with me at the track meet.

She sat with me at the track meet.

Is he free to go with us?

Is he free to go with us?

Part 3
Read the sentences in the box.

1. I will fill this gas can.
2. Can we go to the store?
3. She had a fun trip.

Write the first word of these sentences.

3rd sentence _____ She

1st sentence _____ I

2nd sentence _____ Can

Writing words, copying sentences

Lesson 5   5

Lesson 6

Name _____

Part 1
Copy the sentences.

The junk did not fit in that truck.

The junk did not fit in that truck.

Will Pat feed the cats?

Will Pat feed the cats?

A steep hill had grass on it.

A steep hill had grass on it.

His feet feel sore and cold.

His feet feel sore and cold.

Part 2

(on) linrstanbcs (on) athehlul (on) etack (on) aelinolsd (on) ra (on) a (on) nl e ⑥

(for) on (for) ts (for) ld tote (for) ortal (for) kf ane (for) pkd (for) tasfi ⑥

(to) so (to) dpf osaw (to) keta owalth (to) sh (to) ushtrc (to) jpia (to) eht (to) a ⑦

Part 3
Read the sentences in the box.

1. The man told him, "Hop in this truck."
2. Pat said, "He will feed the cat."
3. She said, "Fill this sack with fish."

Write the first word of these sentences.

2nd sentence _____ Pat

1st sentence _____ The

3rd sentence _____ She

Writing sentences, finding words, writing words

6   *Lesson 6*

121

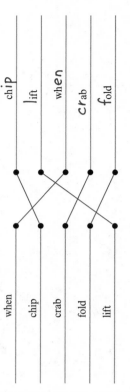

Lesson 8

(ch) oisch ndsndr e h shadth e h esaich wh critheich opshtch — 6

(th) utoth eonisnidch th heptoshttoeth sheto hesth olth r — 5

(ing) kmsdaitoing ratishing t mattomeings cinpisxding er — 4

Name _____

Part 2
Copy the sentences.

She is sending me to the meeting at the shop.

She is sending me to the meeting at the shop.

We do not have the list with us.

We do not have the list with us.

His truck has a bad dent in the top.

His truck has a bad dent in the top.

She ran fast at the track meet.

She ran fast at the track meet.

Part 3
Match the words and complete them.

when	chip
chip	lift
crab	when
fold	crab
lift	fold

Finding letters, writing sentences, matching words

8   *Lesson 8*

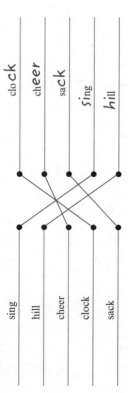

Lesson 7

Name _____

Part 1
Match the words and complete them.

sing	clock
hill	cheer
cheer	sack
clock	sing
sack	hill

Part 2
Read the sentences in the box.

1. Fold that green rag.
2. How much cash do you have?
3. That man has an old cat.

Write the first word of these sentences.

1st sentence   Fold

3rd sentence   That

2nd sentence   How

Part 3
Copy the sentences.

How did she do in the math class?

How did she do in the math class?

That man has more cats than I have.

That man has more cats than I have.

Fill this sack with fish.

Fill this sack with fish.

Will she sell that horse this week?

Will she sell that horse this week?

Writing words, copying sentences

Lesson 7   7

Name _____

Part 1
Read the sentences in the box.

1. When will we win a track meet?
2. They were not singing.
3. Can you sell that truck?

Write the first word of these sentences.

2nd sentence _____ They
3rd sentence _____ Can
1st sentence _____ When

Part 2
Copy the sentences.

The bus went faster than the old truck.

The bus went faster than the old truck.

Which letter did you send her?

Which letter did you send her?

Bring them back to class in the morning.

Bring them back to class in the morning.

That man was the last person on the bus.

That man was the last person on the bus.

Part 3
Match the words and complete them.

shop — much

ranch — shop

much — sheet

lift — ranch

sheet — lift

Lesson 9   9

Writing words, writing sentences, matching words

Name _____

Part 1
Copy the sentences.

Were you in the street after the truck crash?

Were you in the street after the truck crash?

The cat will drink the milk in that pan.

The cat will drink the milk in that pan.

What did that woman tell you to do?

What did that woman tell you to do?

After a nap, he felt much better.

After a nap, he felt much better.

Part 2
Read the sentences in the box.

1. Was she with him when you met her?
2. They sell chips in that store.
3. Bring me that glass of milk.

Write the first word of these sentences.

1st sentence _____ Was
3rd sentence _____ Bring
2nd sentence _____ They

Part 3

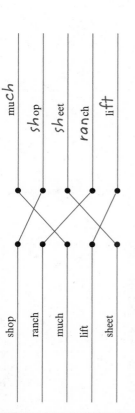

Writing sentences, writing words, finding words

10   *Lesson 10*

123

Lesson 11

Name _____

Part 1
Match the words and complete them.

rancher — p*a*th
going — *sh*elf
path — ranch*er*
shelf — *going*

Part 2
Copy the sentences.

The horse jumped over the creek.

The horse jumped over the creek.

Tim fell into the creek when the horse jumped.

Tim fell into the creek when the horse jumped.

Part 3
of o n f o r t h i s t o p (of) a f t e r p o n d y o y h r s e c o t (of) t o l d o n (of) y ③

said s a n d s i d (said) h a d s a d (said) s l i p s i s a t (said) s l o w s t o p (said) ④

how h o p h o t n o w (how) s h o p f l o w h o p (how) s h o t o w h s l o w c r o w ②

Part 4
Read the sentences in the box.

1. Just then, his sister yelled.
2. Where is the red broom?
3. He told her what to do.

Write the last word of these sentences.

2nd sentence _____ *broom*
3rd sentence _____ *do*
1st sentence _____ *yelled*

Writing words, copying sentences, finding words, writing words

Copyright © SRA/McGraw-Hill. Permission is granted to reproduce for classroom use.

Lesson 11   **11**

Lesson 12

Name _____

Part 1
Read the sentences in the box.

1. Tim went to the trash can.
2. His sister gave orders.
3. He began to sweep.

Write the last word of these sentences.

3rd sentence _____ *sweep*
1st sentence _____ **can**
2nd sentence _____ *orders*

Part 2
Copy the sentences.

Tim got the broom and began to sweep.

Tim got the broom and began to sweep.

He told his sister what to do.

He told his sister what to do.

His sister got mad and yelled at him.

His sister got mad and yelled at him.

Part 3
do t h e t o i t d i m (do) w a s (do) d i d s e e d a (dd) (do) t o l d s i t (do) c l i p i (do) ⑤

one c o r n o f t o d e e r (one) o r o n h i s (one) t o t o r n i t (one) s a (one) n o ④

Part 4
Match the words and complete them.

where — tra*sh*
master — order*s*
trash — mast*er*
orders — *wh*ere

Writing words, copying sentences, finding words, writing words

12   *Lesson 12*

Copyright © SRA/McGraw-Hill. Permission is granted to reproduce for classroom use.

124

Lesson 13

Part 1
Copy the sentences.

What do you think is in this trash can?

What do you think is in this trash can?

She filled a sack with shells.

She filled a sack with shells.

His mom told him what happened.

His mom told him what happened.

Part 2
Read the sentences in the box.

1. These socks go with black slacks.
2. He had red socks for running.
3. His little sister grinned.
4. Ron's mom was not glad.

Write the last word of these sentences.

2nd sentence	running
4th sentence	glad
3rd sentence	grinned
1st sentence	slacks

Part 3
Match the words and complete them.

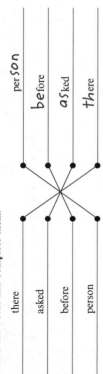

there   per**son**
asked   **b**e**fore**
before   a**s**ked
person   **there**

Lesson 14

Part 1
Read the sentences in the box.

1. Get that ice out of my pocket.
2. At last, she stopped.
3. Now I will help you.
4. How did she do that?

Write the last word of these sentences.

4th sentence	that
2nd sentence	stopped
1st sentence	pocket
3rd sentence	you

Part 2
Match the words and complete them.

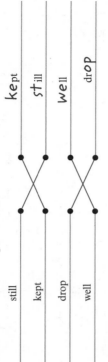

still   **ke**pt
kept   s**t**ill
drop   **we**ll
well   dr**o**p

Part 3
Copy the sentences.

He had a big chunk of ice in his bag.

He had a big chunk of ice in his bag.

She helped the rat hop.

She helped the rat hop.

How do you think she did that?

How do you think she did that?

Lesson 15

Name _____

Part 1

ed) a f t e r e d t u s h e d r l h e r l o e d p n m c v e d w r e r a e d t o u e d b c i e s 6
lie) c h l i d s l i e d i d n o g u m l i e n o t h e l i e s a t l i p l i e l i f t l i e s 5
are) h o w t h e n a n t a r e a n d a r e r e d c a b a t r a m s a r e r a t s a r e a n 4

Part 2

The words in the first column have endings.
Write the same words without endings in the second column.

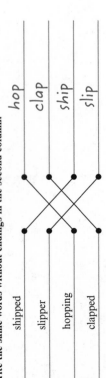

shipped   hop
slipper   clap
hopping   ship
clapped   slip

Part 3

Read the sentences in the box.

1. Sandy went to the store.
2. The rat ate at a fast rate.
3. She gave the rat oats.
4. The rat chomped and chomped.

Write the last word of these sentences.

4th sentence   chomped
1st sentence   store
3rd sentence   oats
2nd sentence   rate

Part 4

Copy the sentence.
She gave the rat oats with gum on them.

She gave the rat oats with gum on them.

Finding words, suffixes, writing words, copying sentences

Lesson 16

Name _____

Part 1

Read the sentences in the box.

1. She got a rat that ate.
2. That rat ate at a fast rate.
3. Sandy dropped the rat into a box.
4. The rat bit Sandy on the nose.

Write the last word of these sentences.

4th sentence   nose
1st sentence   ate
3rd sentence   box
2nd sentence   rate

Part 2

ea) s e e m t o e a h e a r h e a l r a t e h e r e a r s e r a e s t o w e a t c f e a 6
too) c h o f a t o o i e d i d t o o f o r l i e n o t t o o e s a t o o n l i e t o t o o i e s 5
who) h o w t h e n a t a r e w h o m n a r e w h o z c a b e w h o i t y u w h o n g h o w a 4

Part 3

The words in the first column have endings.
Write the same words without endings in the second column.

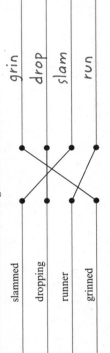

slammed   grin
dropping   drop
runner   slam
grinned   run

Part 4

Copy the sentence.
The fat rat ate oats for seven days.

The fat rat ate oats for seven days.

Writing words, finding words, suffixes, copying sentences

Lesson 16

Name _____

Part 5

The Rat That Had a Fast Rate

Sandy had a rat that ate fast. She said, "That rat eats too   13
much. I must make the rat slow down."   21

Sandy went to the store and got ten packs of gum. She   33
said, "I will smear the gum on the oats." Then she gave the oats   47
to the rat. "Here are some oats," she said. "You will have fun   60
eating them."   62

The rat began eating at a very fast rate. But then the rate   75
began to go down.   79

The rat chomped and chomped. The rat said, "I like oats,   90
but these oats are not fun. I am chomping as fast as I can, but   105
the oats don't go down."   110

Sandy said, "Ho, ho. There is gum on them so that you can   123
not eat at a fast rate."   129

The rat said, "Give me the oats that do not have gum on   142
them, and I will eat slowly."   148

Sandy said, "I am happy to hear that."   156

She gave the rat oats that did not have gum on them. The   169
rat did 2 things. She bit Sandy's hand. Then she ate the oats at a   184
very fast rate.   187

Sandy said, "You little rat. You told me a lie."   197

A Note to the Parent

Listen to the student read the passage. Count the number of words
read in one minute and the number of errors.

Number of words read _____ # _____ Number of errors _____ # _____

We read the story _____ # _____ times.

(Parent's/Listener's signature) _____ Signature

Date _____ Date

Lesson 17

Name _____

Part 1

Copy the sentences.

The camp woman gave him a hammer.

The camp woman gave him a hammer.

She fixed the lamp.

She fixed the lamp.

Can you work better than the rest of us?

Can you work better than the rest of us?

Part 2

The words in the first column have endings.
Write the same words without endings in the second column.

later ———————— time
timing ———————— shape
shaped ———————— hope
hoping ———————— late

Part 3

    a s w h e b t o e a h e a (o a) h e a t (o a) d o o (o a) e a o l (o a) r e e s t (o a) e r u w f (o a) j   ⑥

for   f i l l (for) f e e d s (for) t o r n (for) f o r t o o f s a t (for) l i e a t o f o f i s   ④

make   h o w t h e (make) m a d w h o (make) m a d e i t (make) m a n s   ④

127

Lesson 18

Name _____

Part 1
The words in the first column have endings.
Write the same words without endings in the second column.

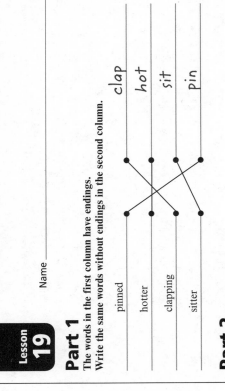

canned	run
hotter	grab
grabbing	can
runner	hot

Part 2
Copy the sentences.

The man with the faster rate will win.

The man with the faster rate will win.

I can even take a bath faster than you.

I can even take a bath faster than you.

Part 3
Match the words and complete them.

their	held
women	th*eir*
held	sh*ow*
show	*wo*men

Part 4

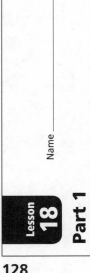

day — a s d a d **day** b a d **day** a t b i d d i d o n d e e r **day** a f t e r **day** d e n ④

bath — back **bath** b a g b i t p a t h **bath** f o r b e d b e a t s a t f o r b e d **bath** b r ③

soon — h o w t h e **soon** t o o **soon** r o o m o f m a k e **soon** b r o o m **soon** s ④

Suffixes, copying sentences, writing words, finding words

Lesson 19

Name _____

Part 1
The words in the first column have endings.
Write the same words without endings in the second column.

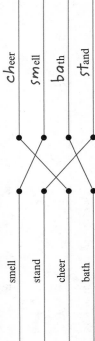

pinned	clap
hotter	hot
clapping	sit
sitter	pin

Part 2
Read the sentences in the box.

1. Champ said, "I am your brother."
2. He said, "You need boaters."
3. The camp woman clapped.

Write the last word of these sentences.

2nd sentence	boaters
1st sentence	brother
3rd sentence	clapped

Part 3
Match the words and complete them.

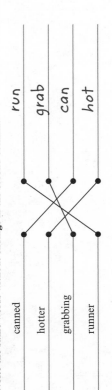
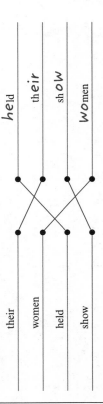

smell	*ch*eer
stand	*s*mell
cheer	b*a*th
bath	*st*and

Part 4
Copy the sentences.

The camp woman held her nose.

The camp woman held her nose.

Bob bent down and began to paddle.

Bob bent down and began to paddle.

Suffixes, writing words, writing sentences

Name _____

Part 1

Read the item and fill in the circle next to the answer. Write the answer in the blank.

1. The con man had a box of ___mops___.

   ○ locks   ○ clocks   ● mops   ○ tops

2. Champ was a fast ___slop___ raker.

   ○ slope   ● slop   ○ shore   ○ shop

3. Champ said, "I will ___prop___ this mop near the door."

   ● prop   ○ slop   ○ stop   ○ bop

4. The con man sold the camp woman a ___bad___ mops.

   ○ seven   ○ thin   ○ 50   ● bad

Part 2

The words in the first column have endings. Write the same words without endings in the second column.

mopping	mop
grabbed	drop
dropper	slip
slipping	grab

Part 3

Copy the sentence.

The con man was glad to sell the mops.

The con man was glad to sell the mops.

Comprehension items, suffixes, copying sentences

Copyright © SRA/McGraw-Hill. Permission is granted to reproduce for classroom use.

Lesson 21   27

Name _____

Part 1

Read the item and fill in the circle next to the answer. Write the answer in the blank.

1. Champ said, "I can not open this door. This door has a ___lock___ on it."

   ○ handle   ○ note   ● lock   ○ top

2. Big Bob said, "I will ___kick___ the door in."

   ○ fix   ● kick   ○ pick   ○ lock

3. The old man held a ___horn___ to his ear.

   ○ pick   ○ handle   ● horn   ○ top

4. Big Bob said, "Make a ___note___ for the old man."

   ○ clock   ○ lock   ○ horn   ● note

Part 2

The words in the first column have endings. Write the same words without endings in the second column.

later	hope
timing	late
saved	save
hoping	time

Part 3

Copy the sentences.

Champ grabbed the handle of the door.

Champ grabbed the handle of the door.

The old man hit the lock with a hammer.

The old man hit the lock with a hammer.

Directions, Part 1: Read the directions to the student. "Read the item and fill in the circle next to the answer. Write the answer in the blank."

Copyright © SRA/McGraw-Hill. Permission is granted to reproduce for classroom use.

Lesson 20   25

Lesson 23

Name _____

Part 1

The words in the first column have endings.
Write the same words without endings in the second column.

slammed — sit

dropping — clap

sitter — slam

clapped — drop

Part 2

Read the sentence and fill in the circle next to the answer.
Write the answer in the blank.

1. When Gretta said, "Ho, ho," Chee __became very mad__.

   ○ made a note   ○ sat near the door   ● became very mad

2. Chee asked Gretta, "Did you __have fun__ at your job?"

   ○ work fast   ○ feel sad   ● have fun   ○ sell fish

Part 3

Copy the sentences.

She got better and better at saying things.

She got better and better at saying things.

I don't like to stay at home.

I don't like to stay at home.

He will get a job, too.

He will get a job, too.

Suffixes, comprehension items, copying sentences

Copyright © SRA/McGraw-Hill. Permission is granted to reproduce for classroom use.

Lesson 23   31

Lesson 22

Name _____

Part 1

Match the words and complete them.

matter — be cause

because — sha ck

lifted — lift ed

shack — mat ter

Part 2

Copy the sentences.

Cathy worked in a dress shop.

Cathy worked in a dress shop.

Cathy and Pam left the shed and sat on a bench.

Cathy and Pam left the shed and sat on a bench.

Part 3

Read the item and fill in the circle next to the answer.
Write the answer in the blank.

1. Pam led Cathy to a __fish shed__.

   ○ dress shop   ○ big camp   ○ clock store   ● fish shed

2. The man in a big coat said, "I am a __fish packer__."

   ○ cook   ○ worker   ● fish packer   ○ slop raker

3. The man had a basket of fish in his __boat__.

   ○ shed   ● boat   ○ shop   ○ store

4. The man in the fish shed gave Pam and Cathy __free__ chips.

   ● free   ○ five   ○ fish   ○ flat

Writing words, copying sentences, comprehension items

Copyright © SRA/McGraw-Hill. Permission is granted to reproduce for classroom use.

Lesson 22   29

130

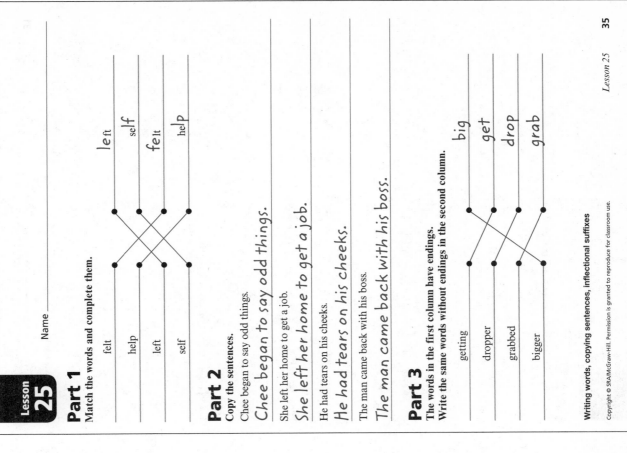

Lesson 25

Name _____

Part 1
Match the words and complete them.

felt   le**ft**

help   se**lf**

left   fe**lt**

self   he**lp**

Part 2
Copy the sentences.

Chee began to say odd things.

Chee began to say odd things.

She left her home to get a job.

She left her home to get a job.

He had tears on his cheeks.

He had tears on his cheeks.

The man came back with his boss.

The man came back with his boss.

Part 3
The words in the first column have endings.
Write the same words without endings in the second column.

getting   big

dropper   get

grabbed   drop

bigger   grab

Writing words, copying sentences, inflectional suffixes

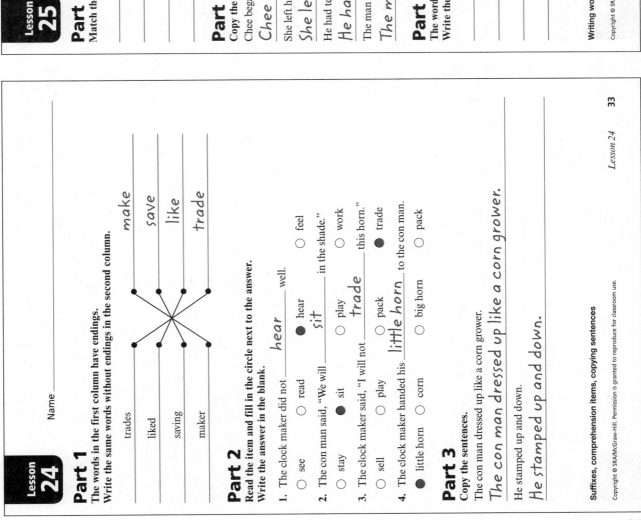

Lesson 24

Name _____

Part 1
The words in the first column have endings.
Write the same words without endings in the second column.

trades   make

liked   save

saving   like

maker   trade

Part 2
Read the item and fill in the circle next to the answer.
Write the answer in the blank.

1. The clock maker did not ___hear___ well.
   ○ see   ○ read   ● hear   ○ feel

2. The con man said, "We will ___sit___ in the shade."
   ○ stay   ● sit   ○ play   ○ work

3. The clock maker said, "I will not ___trade___ this horn."
   ○ sell   ○ play   ○ pack   ● trade

4. The clock maker handed his ___little horn___ to the con man.
   ● little horn   ○ corn   ○ big horn   ○ pack

Part 3
Copy the sentences.

The con man dressed up like a corn grower.

The con man dressed up like a corn grower.

He stamped up and down.

He stamped up and down.

Suffixes, comprehension items, copying sentences

Lesson 26

Part 1
Read the words in the box. Then fill in the blanks.

worked	well	rode	named	fast
good	best	swam	ran	bent

There was a ranch in the West. The rancher who __ran__ this ranch was named __named__ Emma Branch. She rode a horse __well__. She chopped __fast__, and she swam faster. The men and women who __worked__ for Emma Branch liked her. They said, "She is the best in the West."

Part 2
The words in the first column have endings.
Write the same words without endings in the second column.

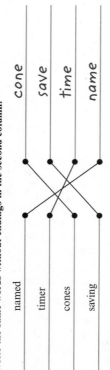

named   cone

timer   save

cones   time

saving   name

Part 3
Copy the sentences.

She checked up on the workers.
She checked up on the workers.

Get ready to leave now.
Get ready to leave now.

This horse is very tame.
This horse is very tame.

Vocabulary/context clues, suffixes, copying sentences

Name _____

Lesson 27

Part 1
Read the words in the box. Then fill in the blanks.

fastest	packer	stick	plant	old
stackers	slowest	odd	mad	slate
pack	made	slat	job	stack

Chee got a __job__ at a __slate__ plant. When she was not __mad__, she did not say __odd__ things. The woman who ran the __plant__ showed Chee how to __stack__ slate. At the end of one year, Chee was one of the fastest __stackers__.

Part 2
Copy the sentences.

The woman showed Chee how to stack slate.
The woman showed Chee how to stack slate.

She worked at the plant for nearly a year.
She worked at the plant for nearly a year.

Set that slab on top of the pile.
Set that slab on top of the pile.

Part 3
The words in the first column have endings.
Write the same words without endings in the second column.

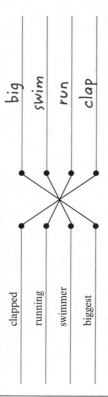

clapped   big

running   swim

swimmer   run

biggest   clap

Vocabulary/context clues, copying sentences, suffixes

Name _____

Part 1
Read the words in the box. Then fill in the blanks.

tamps	ranch	rest	pack	old
odd	slop	camp	say	stay
sack	ramps	hill	lake	leave

Champ worked at the ___camp___ for nearly a year. He tamped and made ___ramps___.

Now he said, "I will ___leave___ this camp. Champs don't ___stay___ in a camp for more than a year."

So Champ got his ___pack___. He told the camp woman, "The work here is getting ___old___, and I need a ___rest___."

Part 2
The words in the first column have endings.
Write the same words without endings in the second column.

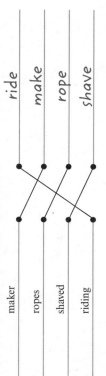

maker	ride
ropes	make
shaved	rope
riding	shave

Part 3
Copy the sentences.

He worked there for nearly a year.
He worked there for nearly a year.

When the sun comes up, he will shear sheep.
When the sun comes up, he will shear sheep.

Vocabulary/context clues, suffixes, copying sentences

Lesson 29   43

Name _____

Part 1
Read the words in the box. Then fill in the blanks.

leave	shop	sheep	sacks	best
steal	work	shave	plan	faster
packs	shears	wool	well	fake

The con man said, "I can ___shave___ a sheep before it sees the ___shears___. You can ___shop___, but you cannot get someone who can shave ___faster___ than me."

The con man told the rancher to get him ten ___sacks___ for holding the ___wool___. He did not plan to shear ___sheep___. He planned to ___steal___ them.

Part 2
Match the words and complete them.

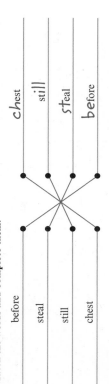

before	chest
steal	still
still	steal
chest	before

Part 3
Copy the sentences.

He got the shears from his pack.
He got the shears from his pack.

He planned to pack sheep into sacks.
He planned to pack sheep into sacks.

The rancher sat on the con man and shaved his locks.
The rancher sat on the con man and shaved his locks.

Vocabulary/context clues, writing words, copying sentences

Lesson 28   41

134

Lesson 30

Name _____

Part 1
Read the item and fill in the circle next to the answer.
Write the answer in the blank.

1. Champ was sleeping near a sheep ___shed___ .
   ○ camp   ● shed   ○ shop   ○ ranch

2. Champ felt more like ___sleeping___ than shearing.
   ○ sweeping   ○ shaving   ○ yelling   ● sleeping

3. Emma said, "You have ___50___ minutes to shear ___50___ sheep."
   ○ five   ● 50   ○ 20   ○ ten

4. Emma kept her ___deal___ with Champ.
   ○ plan   ○ ranch   ● deal   ○ hand

Part 2
Copy the sentences.

The sun came up in the morning.

The sun came up in the morning.

The cook will make a good meal.

The cook will make a good meal.

Part 3
The words in the first column have endings.
Write the same words without endings in the second column.

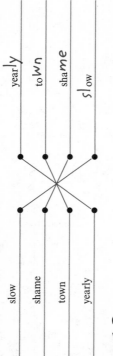

sweeping   help

reached   reach

helper   sweep

Comprehension items, copying sentences, suffixes

Lesson 30   **45**

Copyright © SRA/McGraw-Hill. Permission is granted to reproduce for classroom use.

Lesson 31

Name _____

Part 1
Match the words and complete them.

slow   year**ly**

shame   to**wn**

town   sha**me**

yearly   s**l**ow

Part 2
Copy the sentences.

He got slower and slower with each meal that he ate.

He got slower and slower with each meal that he ate.

Emma went to town and bragged.

Emma went to town and bragged.

Part 3
Read the words in the box. Then fill in the blanks.

like	rested	said	mean	time
best	look	shave	shape	shade
bad	meet	good	neat	seem

The rancher said, "We will have the ___meet___ at the end of this week. So get in ___shape___ ."

"Yes, yes," the fat champ said.

"I ___mean___ it," the rancher said. "You ___seem___ to be in ___bad___ shape. You have ___rested___ for seven weeks. Now you don't ___look___ like you can do things very fast."

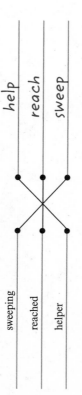

Writing words, copying sentences, vocabulary/context clues

Lesson 31   **47**

Copyright © SRA/McGraw-Hill. Permission is granted to reproduce for classroom use.

Lesson 32

Part 1
Read the item and fill in the circle next to the answer.
Write the answer in the blank.

1. Shelly made a ___heap___ of wool as big as a hill.
   ○ pack ● heap ○ sheer ○ sweep

2. Champ made a pile of wool as big as a ___little___ sheep.
   ● little ○ fatter ○ big ○ short

3. Emma said to Champ, "You will ___work___ like a horse."
   ○ run ○ go ○ rest ● work

4. Champ had never been ___beaten___ in a meet before.
   ○ shaved ● beaten ○ broken ○ picked

Part 2
The words in the first column have endings.
Write the same words without endings in the second column.

melted — work
working — melt
beaten — slow
slower — beat

Part 3
Copy the sentences.
She showed the others how fast she was.
She showed the others how fast she was.

He ate big meals of ham and beans.
He ate big meals of ham and beans.

Comprehension items, inflectional suffixes, copying sentences

Lesson 32 49

Lesson 33

Part 1
The words in the first column have endings.
Write the same words without endings in the second column.

beginning — plant
planter — begin
peeking — work
worked — peek

Part 2
Read the words in the box. Then fill in the blanks.

shaping	shaving	faster	week	work
fatter	sore	sheared	hot	meals
cold	hands	hammer	made	shape

The rancher gave Champ more work. At the end of the day, Champ was ___sore___.

But at the end of the week, he began to get ___faster___. His ___hammer___ began to go like a flash. His shears began to get ___hot___ when he was ___shaving___ sheep. Champ was beginning to get back in ___shape___.

Part 3
Copy the sentences.
His hammer began to go like a flash.
His hammer began to go like a flash.

There was no more work at the ranch.
There was no more work at the ranch.

Suffixes, vocabulary/context clues, copying sentences

Lesson 33 51

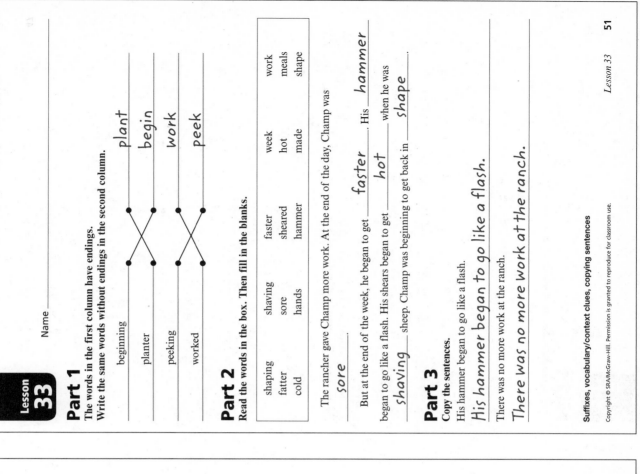

136

Lesson 34

Name _____

Part 1
Read the item and fill in the circle next to the answer.
Write the answer in the blank.

1. Shelly said, "I have never been ___beaten___ in a shearing meet."
   ○ broken   ○ cheered   ● beaten   ○ shaved

2. At the end of the meet, Champ had sheared ___9,000___ sheep.
   ○ 5,000   ● 9,000   ○ 210   ○ 501

3. Shelly had sheared ___501___ sheep.
   ○ 5,000   ○ 9,000   ○ 210   ● 501

Part 2
The words in the first column have endings.
Write the same words without endings in the second column.

cheered ——— *pant*
panting ——— *ranch*
beaten ——— *cheer*
rancher ——— *beat*

Part 3
Copy the sentences.

She is the best worker at the plant.
She is the best worker at the plant.

The people from town waved to Champ.
The people from town waved to Champ.

Her helpers began to bag the wool.
Her helpers began to bag the wool.

Comprehension items, suffixes, copying sentences

Lesson 35

Name _____

Part 1
Read the words in the box. Then fill in the blanks.

day	packer	speed	rate	packing	plant
quit	week	stacking	year	shearing	rat
stacker	shack	leave	slacks	sick	time

Chee worked as a slate ___stacker___ for nearly a year. By then, her ___rate___ of ___stacking___ was very good. But she was getting a little ___sick___ of her job. "Stack, stack, stack," she said. "It's time to do something else." So she went to the woman who ran the slate ___plant___ and said, "I think I have to ___quit___ and get another job."

Part 2
The words in the first column have endings.
Write the same words without endings in the second column.

waited ——— *near*
stacker ——— *wait*
seated ——— *seat*
nearly ——— *stack*

Part 3
Match the words and complete them.

something ——— some*thing*
person ——— *yel*low
yellow ——— *coa*ts
coats ——— *per*son

Vocabulary/context, inflectional suffixes, writing words

Name _____

Part 1
Cross out the words that don't have ea.

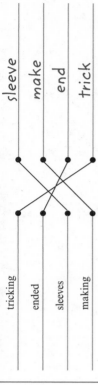

~~rain~~	mean	hear	each	~~sleep~~
shear	~~began~~	~~these~~	~~steal~~	beat
seating	real	~~real~~	~~between~~	reach

Part 2
Read the words in the box. Then fill in the blanks.

tricking	slapped	lap	sleeves
stammer	making	slabs	slap
stabbed	coats	fast	score
			handed
			store
			wool

Chee and Rop went into the sleeve- _making_ room of the plant. There

Rop said, "I will get the best _score_ for this meet. We will see how fast that

lap dog can slap sleeves in _coats_ . The dog that slaps sleeves

fastest will win."

Rop _handed_ Chee a needle. Chee went very fast, but she _stabbed_

herself with the needle.

Part 3
The words in the first column have endings.
Write the same words without endings in the second column.

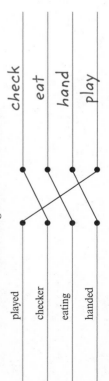

tricking _____ _sleeve_

ended _____ _make_

sleeves _____ _end_

making _____ _trick_

Sound/symbol correspondence, vocabulary/context clues, inflectional suffixes

---

Name _____

Part 1
Read the words in the box. Then fill in the blanks.

eat	slop	run	ran	slabs	see
fish	work	yellow	meat	pick	chomp
fresh	sleeve	meet	sheet	better	score

Chee had met a _yellow_ dog in a _sleeve_ plant. The dog was

named Rop, and he _ran_ the plant. He said that he was _better_

than Chee at doing things. Chee got mad. So a _meet_ was set between Rop

and Chee.

Rop said, "We will begin by seeing how fast we can _eat_ ."

Rop told a worker, "Get me 2 _slabs_ of fresh meat."

Part 2
The words in the first column have endings.
Write the same words without endings in the second column.

played _____ _check_

checker _____ _eat_

eating _____ _hand_

handed _____ _play_

Part 3
Copy the sentences.

She told the best joke.

She told the best joke.

Chee began to stammer and say odd things.

Chee began to stammer and say odd things.

Vocabulary/context clues, inflectional suffixes, copying sentences

138

Name _____

Part 1
The words in the first column have endings.
Write the same words without endings in the second column.

turned
drained
faster
biggest
thinner

thin
fast
drain
turn
big

Part 2
Write the words.

can + not = cannot
any + body = anybody
my + self = myself
some + one = someone

Part 3
Copy the sentences.

He sold gas at the boat ramp.
He sold gas at the boat ramp.

She did not hear waves on the shore.
She did not hear waves on the shore.

Inflectional suffixes, compound words, copying sentences

Name _____

Part 1
Cross out the words that don't have ee.

steered ~~meat~~ ~~boot~~ feel sleep
cheer ~~begun~~ sleeve ~~smell~~ ~~beat~~
~~seating~~ wheel ~~nock~~ between steel

Part 2
Write the words.

any + one = anyone
some + body = somebody
her + self = herself
down + hill = downhill

Part 3
Copy the sentences.

The boat was in the middle of the sea.
The boat was in the middle of the sea.

The goat ate a hole in the boat.
The goat ate a hole in the boat.

Part 4
The words in the first column have endings.
Write the same words without endings in the second column.

holes   order
baking   hole
ordered   bake

Sound/symbol correspondence, compound words, copying sentences, inflectional suffixes

Lesson 41

Name _____

Part 1
Write the words.

good + bye = _goodbye_
no + thing = _nothing_
any + body = _anybody_
down + hill = _downhill_
six + teen = _sixteen_

Part 2
Read the words in the box. Then fill in the blanks.

sail	boat	nobody	light	aim	white
bike	save	yellow	nothing	green	slow
red	sell	send	steak	pain	float

Kit said, "I am going to _sell_ this boat and get a _bike_.
This boat is _nothing_ but a _pain_."
Then she said to herself, "I can have a lot of fun with a bike. If I get a bike, it will be very _light_, so I'll fly over town."

Part 3
Cross out the words that don't have ol.

~~boat~~   told   ~~boat~~   cold   fold   ~~loading~~
~~float~~   ~~began~~   old   ~~meat~~   bolted

Compound words, vocabulary/context clues, sound/symbol correspondence

Copyright © SRA/McGraw-Hill. Permission is granted to reproduce for classroom use.

Lesson 41   67

Lesson 40

Name _____

Part 1
The words in the first column have endings.
Write the same words without endings in the second column.

sleeves — _cut_
cutter — _sleeve_
waited — _make_
making — _wait_

Part 2
Cross out the words that don't have oa.

~~goat~~   ~~mean~~   boat   ~~book~~   loading
~~float~~   ~~these~~   board   coat   ~~beat~~

Part 3
Write the words.

an + other = _another_
some + one = _someone_

Part 4
Read the item and fill in the circle next to the answer.
Write the answer in the blank.

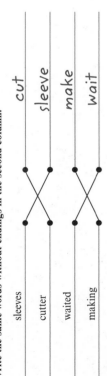

1. Kit put rocks in the _front_ of her boat.
   ○ back   ● front   ○ top   ○ side

2. Kit said, "Things go fast when they go _downhill_."
   ○ closer   ○ faster   ● downhill   ○ through

3. The boat made a hole in the _side_ of the bank.
   ○ back   ○ front   ○ slide   ● side

Suffixes, sound/symbol correspondence, compound words, comprehension items

Copyright © SRA/McGraw-Hill. Permission is granted to reproduce for classroom use.

Lesson 40   65

139

140

Lesson 42

Name _____

Part 1
Cross out the words that don't have **sh.**

shape   ~~with~~   shift   ~~chest~~
~~which~~   ~~chop~~   fish   ~~what~~   ~~cheer~~

Part 2
The words in the first column have endings.
Write the same words without endings in the second column.

boating ——— take
opened ——— stroke
stroked ——— boat
taken ——— open

Part 3
Write the words.

every + thing = _everything_
through + out = _throughout_
good + bye = _goodbye_
with + out = _without_

Part 4
Copy the sentences.
The shop man looked at the motor.

The shop man looked at the motor.

She handed three books to him.

She handed three books to him.

Sound/symbol correspondence, inflectional suffixes, compound words, copying sentences

Copyright © SRA/McGraw-Hill. Permission is granted to reproduce for classroom use.

Lesson 42   **69**

Lesson 43

Name _____

Part 1
Write the words.

door + way = _doorway_
home + work = _homework_
no + thing = _nothing_
some + one = _someone_

Part 2
Cross out the words that don't have **ck.**

~~cash~~   packing   ~~clapped~~   clocks   ~~creek~~   mean   roar
rocked   neck   ~~chops~~   ~~picked~~   black   grabbed   worker
                                                  reader   words

Part 3
Read the words in the box. Then fill in the blanks.

jumped	saw	bolts	tossed
tore	need	smiled	rod
fixed	whispered	motor	rubbed

Molly said, "Here is the book. It tells where everything is on the _motor_ .
Read the book, and it will tell you what you _need_ to know."

So Molly went to the street and _jumped_ into her hot rod. She
grabbed the wheel, and she _tore_ down the street.

Henry took his book and _whispered_ to himself, "I wish I was a better
reader ."

Compound words, sound/symbol correspondence, vocabulary/context clues

Copyright © SRA/McGraw-Hill. Permission is granted to reproduce for classroom use.

Lesson 43   **71**

Lesson 45

Name _____

Part 1
Write the words.

some + body = _somebody_
up + set = _upset_
with + out = _without_
door + way = _doorway_

Part 2
The words in the first column have endings.
Write the same words without endings in the second column.

trenches   _real_
fishing   _trade_
really   _trench_
traded   _fish_

Part 3
Read the words in the box. Then fill in the blanks.

rested	tires	sell	ripped	site	grip
crime	bikes	rid	roads	gripe	deal
conned	steal	ships	ready	paths	robbed

Kit said, "I think I will get _rid_ of this boat. It makes _ships_ sink. It has _ripped_ up 2 docks. It has made _paths_ and trenches. It tore holes in the bank, and that is a bad _crime_,"

Kit had a lot to _gripe_ over. So she said, "I will _sell_ the boat."

Compound words, suffixes, vocabulary/context clues

Lesson 44

Name _____

Part 1
The words in the first column have endings.
Write the same words without endings in the second column.

dragging   _toss_
timing   _time_
saying   _drag_
tossed   _say_

Part 2
Write the words.

some + body = _somebody_
up + side = _upside_
with + out = _without_
down + town = _downtown_

Part 3
Read the item and fill in the circle next to the answer.
Write the answer in the blank.

1. Henry was trying to fix a broken cam ___shaft___.
   ○ shift   ● shaft   ○ stack

2. After a while, his motor was in little ___bits___.
   ○ gears   ● bits   ○ rods

3. Molly fixed her hot rod because she was able to ___read___.
   ○ work   ○ know   ○ bolt   ○ bolts   ● read

Inflectional suffixes, compound words, comprehension items

142

Lesson 46

Name _____

Part 1
Read the words in the box. Then fill in the blanks.

faster	really	lifted	ready	sold	worker
tires	fastest	robber	diver	zip	float
bikes	traded	back	pile	nose	slower

The con man had __traded__ his clock, his cash, his ring, and five
__tires__ with holes in them for Kit's tin boat.

Now the con man was __ready__ to become the best bank __robber__
in the west. He said, "I will __pile__ rocks in the __nose__ of this
boat. The more rocks I pile, the __faster__ it will go."

Part 2
Match the words and complete them.

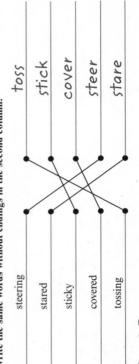

covered   rock et
rocket   idea
zipped   co vered
idea   zip ped

Part 3
**The words in the first column have endings.
Write the same words without endings in the second column.**

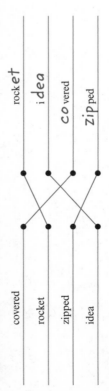

diver   lift
looked   fly
flying   look
lifted   dive

Vocabulary/context clues, writing words, suffixes

Lesson 46   77

Copyright © SRA/McGraw-Hill. Permission is granted to reproduce for classroom use.

Lesson 47

Name _____

Part 1
**Write 1, 2, or 3 in front of each sentence to show when these things happened in the story.
Then write the sentences in the blanks.**

2   The cops and their nine dogs ran up to the con man.

1   The con man was sticking to the seat of the boat.

3   The con man said, "This is a space ship, and I come from space."

1. The con man was sticking to the seat of the boat.

2. The cops and their nine dogs ran up to the con man.

3. The con man said, "This is a space ship, and I come
from space."

Part 2
**The words in the first column have endings.
Write the same words without endings in the second column.**

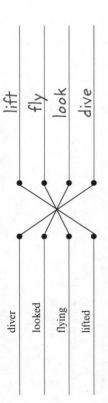

steering   toss
stared   stick
sticky   cover
covered   steer
tossing   stare

Part 3
Copy the sentences.

She is the woman who runs the cotton mill.
She is the woman who runs the cotton mill.

Slowly he began to stand up.
Slowly he began to stand up.

Sequence, suffixes, copying sentences

Lesson 47   79

Copyright © SRA/McGraw-Hill. Permission is granted to reproduce for classroom use.

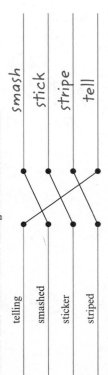

Lesson 49

Name _____

Part 1
Write the word **trying**. Make a line over **ing**. trying

Write the word **moaned**. Make a line under **ed**. moaned

Part 2
The words in the first column have endings.
Write the same words without endings in the second column.

training — smile
tired — jail
smiling — train
jailer — tire

Part 3
Read the words in the box. Then fill in the blanks.

yelling	three	grain	seven	hair	pike
five	hard	slipped	rain	thing	leg
slapped	griping	drained	steps	trying	nose
raining	tired	light	jumped	drain	like

It was _raining_ and the con man was _griping_ about the _rain_. He said, "My plan is going down the _drain_." He was trying to run with _three_ bags of gold, but they were not _light_. He did not run fast. The cotton in his _hair_ was running down his _nose_. He did not see where he was going. He slipped in a pile of slippery _pike_ and fell down.

Part 4
Copy the sentence. They began to lick the taffy.

They began to lick the taffy.

Sound/symbol correspondence, inflectional suffixes, vocabulary/context clues, copying sentences

Lesson 49 83

Lesson 48

Name _____

Part 1
The words in the first column have endings.
Write the same words without endings in the second column.

telling — smash
smashed — stick
sticker — stripe
striped — tell

Part 2
Write the words.

boat + load = boatload
home + work = homework
through + out = throughout

Part 3
Write **1, 2,** or **3** in front of each sentence to show when these things happened in the story. Then write the sentences in the blanks.

3 The con man began to run with the bags of gold, but he did not run very fast.
2 The con man took bags of gold from the bank.
1 The con man said, "I am from space, and I will get you."

1. The con man said, "I am from space, and I will get you."

2. The con man took bags of gold from the bank.

3. The con man began to run with the bags of gold, but he did not run very fast.

Suffixes, compound words, sequence

Lesson 48 81

143

144

Lesson 50

Name _____

Part 1

Write the word **digging**. Make a line over **ing**. ___digging___

Write the word **lower**. Make a line under **er**. ___lower___

Part 2

Write **1, 2,** or **3** in front of each sentence to show when these things happened in the story. Then write the sentences in the blanks.

___3___ The other bugs gave the dusty bug a dime to stay in the cool mine.

___1___ The bugs went inside a big hole to be in a cool spot.

___2___ The mother bug saw the dusty bug digging.

1. _The bugs went inside a big hole to be in a cool spot._

2. _The mother bug saw the dusty bug digging._

3. _The other bugs gave the dusty bug a dime to stay in the cool mine._

Part 3

The words in the first column have endings. Write the same words without endings in the second column.

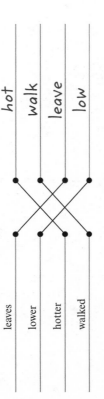

leaves ___hot___

lower ___walk___

hotter ___leave___

walked ___low___

Lesson **51**

Name _____

Part 1

Read the item and fill in the circle next to the answer. Write the answer in the blank.

1. The dusty bug liked ___dills___ .
   ○ bills ○ shovels ● dills ○ smells

2. The bug said, "I don't have ___cash___ with me."
   ○ pickles ● cash ○ tubs ○ mine

3. The bug dug into the ___tub___ and got a big pickle.
   ○ store ○ bag ○ mine ● tub

Part 2

Write the word **outside**. Make a line over **out.** ___out̄side___

Write the word **another**. Make a line under **er.** ___anoth̲er___

Part 3

Match the words and complete them.

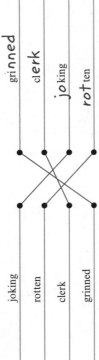

joking   gri nned

rotten   cl erk

clerk   jo king

grinned   rot ten

Part 4

Copy the sentence.

The dusty bug smiled from the door of the store.

The dusty bug smiled from the door of the store.

Lesson 53

Part 1

Write **1**, **2**, or **3** in front of each sentence to show when these things happened in the story. Then write the sentences in the blanks.

2 The clock maker slapped a bell into the deer clock.

1 The clock maker painted the deer yellow.

3 The woman tossed the clock down, and it broke into parts.

1. *The clock maker painted the deer yellow.*

2. *The clock maker slapped a bell into the deer clock.*

3. *The woman tossed the clock down, and it broke into parts.*

Part 2

The words in the first column have endings.
Write the same words without endings in the second column.

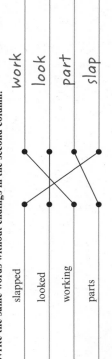

slapped   work
looked   look
working   part
parts   slap

Part 3

Write the word **himself**. Make a line over **self**.   *himself*

Write the word **dabbed**. Make a line under **ed**.   *dabbed*

Part 4

Copy the sentence.

A woman was standing near the door. _____

Sequence, inflectional suffixes, sound/symbol correspondence

Lesson 53   **91**

Lesson 52

Part 1

Match the words and complete them.

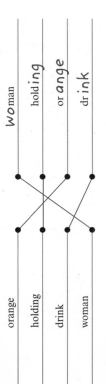

orange   *wo*man
holding   hold*ing*
drink   or*ange*
woman   dr*ink*

Part 2

Read the words in the box. Then fill in the blanks.

table	grabbed	stopped	bib	fixed	binging
taken	broken	dropped	cheer	deer	door
dropping	floor	fixing	making	sound	leak

The clock maker _grabbed_ the clock and _dropped_ it. The clock made a loud _sound_ when it hit the _floor_ . The _deer_ fell out. A spring went, "bop." The clock went, "bing, bing, ding." The clock maker said, "That clock is _broken_ . Let me make a bid on _fixing_ it."

Part 3

Write the words.

ding + ing = _dinging_

real + ly = _really_

sleep + ing = _sleeping_

loud + ly = _loudly_

Writing words, vocabulary/context clues, suffixes

Lesson 52   **89**

Lesson 54

Name _____

Part 1
Write the words.

every + thing = _everything_
with + out = _without_
door + way = _doorway_
out + side = _outside_

Part 2
Write 1, 2, or 3 in front of each sentence to show when these things happened in the story.
Then write the sentences in the blanks.

___3___ The old clock maker took the clock back to the woman.
___1___ An alligator ran across the front of the clock and bit the clock maker's finger.
___2___ The clock maker stuck antlers on the alligator and slapped it into the deer clock.

1. _An alligator ran across the front of the clock and bit the clock maker's finger._

2. _The clock maker stuck antlers on the alligator and slapped it into the deer clock._

3. _The old clock maker took the clock back to the woman._

Part 3
The words in the first column have endings.
Write the same words without endings in the second column.

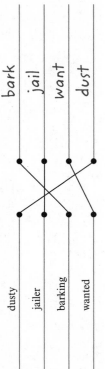

painted — antler
broken — broke
antlers — bust
busted — paint

Lesson 54   **93**

Compound words, sequence, inflectional suffixes

Lesson 55

Name _____

Part 1
Copy the sentences.

The woman tossed the clock into a tree.
The woman tossed the clock into a tree.

A little yellow bird sat on the alligator's antlers.
A little yellow bird sat on the alligator's antlers.

Part 2
The words in the first column have endings.
Write the same words without endings in the second column.

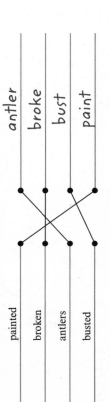

dusty — bark
jailer — jail
barking — want
wanted — dust

Part 3
Read the words in the box. Then fill in the blanks.

third	home	first	next	stayed	way
leaves	time	came	come	bees	house
pay	play	buy	days	birds	trees

The woman said, "For some _time_ , I've wanted to get those _birds_ into my tree, but this is the _first_ time they've _come_ to the tree. Thank you. How can I _pay_ you?"

"Hand me eleven dollars, and I'll be on my _way_ this day," the clock maker said. So the woman gave the clock maker eleven dollars, and he went _home_ .

Lesson 55   **95**

Copying sentences, suffixes, vocabulary/context clues

Lesson 56

Name _____

Part 1

Write **1, 2,** or **3** in front of each sentence to show when these things happened in the story. Then write the sentences in the blanks.

3 The doctor said, "Lock this man up."

2 The bus took the con man to the rest home.

1 The con man got down on the floor and growled at the nurse.

1. The con man got down on the floor and growled at the nurse.

2. The bus took the con man to the rest home.

3. The doctor said, "Lock this man up."

Part 2

The words in the first column have endings.
Write the same words without endings in the second column.

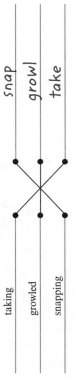

taking

growled

snapping

snap

growl

take

Part 3

Match the words and complete them.

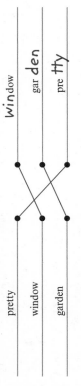

pretty

window

garden

win dow

gar den

pre tty

Sequence, inflectional suffixes, writing words

Copyright © SRA/McGraw-Hill. Permission is granted to reproduce for classroom use.

Lesson 56   97

Lesson 57

Name _____

Part 1

Write the words.

be   +   fore   =   before

some   +   where   =   somewhere

any   +   one   =   anyone

your   +   self   =   yourself

out   +   side   =   outside

Part 2

Copy the sentences.

He tried to get out the window.

He tried to get out the window.

They looked around and didn't see anybody.

They looked around and didn't see anybody.

The doctor took notes on a pad.

The doctor took notes on a pad.

Part 3

Write the name of the person each sentence tells about.

president   con man

1. This person had to be a private in the army.   con man

2. This person said, "You must do everything I say."   president

3. This person marched and marched and marched.   con man

Compound words, copying sentences, characterization

Copyright © SRA/McGraw-Hill. Permission is granted to reproduce for classroom use.

Lesson 57   99

148

Lesson 58

Name _____

Part 1

Write the word **wheat**. Make a line over **ea.** _wheat_

Write the word **hiding**. Make a line under **ing.** _hiding_

Part 2

The words in the first column have endings.
Write the same words without endings in the second column.

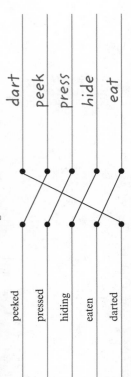

peeked	dart
pressed	peek
hiding	press
eaten	hide
darted	eat

Part 3

Write **1, 2,** or **3** in front of each sentence to show when these things happened in the story.
Then write the sentences in the blanks.

2 The president began to scream, "Oh, my foot. It is stuck in the gate."

1 The con man and the president hid under the bed.

3 The man who ran the gate pressed the button, and the gate opened.

1. _The con man and the president hid under the bed._

2. _The president began to scream, "Oh, my foot. It is stuck in the gate."_

3. _The man who ran the gate pressed the button, and the gate opened._

Writing words, inflectional suffixes, sequence

Lesson 58 **101**

Lesson 59

Name _____

Part 1

Write the words.

near + by = _nearby_

with + out = _without_

be + cause = _because_

loud + ly = _loudly_

Part 2

Write **1, 2,** or **3** in front of each sentence to show when these things happened in the story.
Then write the sentences in the blanks.

3 The president said very loudly, "We are from the bug company."

2 The woman in the main office said, "Take the green car in front of the office."

1 The con man and the president dressed in white jackets and left the shack.

1. _The con man and the president dressed in white jackets and left the shack._

2. _The woman in the main office said, "Take the green car in front of the office."_

3. _The president said very loudly, "We are from the bug company."_

Part 3

The words in the first column have endings.
Write the same words without endings in the second column.

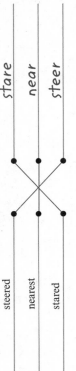

steered	stare
nearest	near
stared	steer

Compound words, sequence, inflectional suffixes

Lesson 59 **103**

Lesson 60

Name _____

Part 1
Cross out the words that don't have **ar**.

chart   alarm   ~~scram~~   ~~drain~~   started   ~~taking~~

army   ~~stream~~   darted   charge   ~~track~~   sharp

Part 2
Write the name of the person each sentence tells about.

president   con man

1. This person said, "I need something to eat."   president
2. This person ordered a big lunch for two.   con man
3. This person said, "I must get away from this guy."   con man
4. This person rolled right off the side of the bed.   president
5. This person said, "Just charge it to the room."   president
6. This person smiled and said, "Tee, hee."   con man

Part 3
The words in the first column have endings.
Write the same words without endings in the second column.

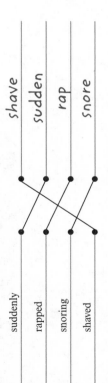

suddenly — sudden
rapped — rap
snoring — snore
shaved — shave

(shave)
(sudden)
(rap)
(snore)

Sound/symbol correspondence, characterization, suffixes

Copyright © SRA/McGraw-Hill. Permission is granted to reproduce for classroom use.

Lesson 60   105

Lesson 61

Name _____

Part 1
Write the word **hamburger**. Make a line over **er**.   hambur̄ger

Write the word **please**. Make a line under **ea**.   pleas̲e

Part 2
Write **1**, **2**, or **3** in front of each sentence to show when these things happened in the story.
Then write the sentences in the blanks.

2 — The president said to the man behind the desk, "Give me my money back."

1 — The president cut some hair from the man's wig and made a beard with it.

3 — The president and the con man got into a cab and drove away.

1. The president cut some hair from the man's wig and made a beard with it.

2. The president said to the man behind the desk, "Give me my money back."

3. The president and the con man got into a cab and drove away.

Part 3
Write the name of the person each sentence tells about.

president   con man   man at the desk

1. This person began to tell a story about a battle.   president
2. This person said, "We must escape."   president
3. This person said, "Well, let's dash, buster."   con man
4. This person said that there were bugs in the hotel.   president
5. This person handed over two hundred dollars.   man at the desk

Sound/symbol correspondence, sequence, characterization

Copyright © SRA/McGraw-Hill. Permission is granted to reproduce for classroom use.

Lesson 61   107

Lesson 62

Name _____

Part 1
The words in the first column have endings.
Write the same words without endings in the second column.

marching — bright
brightness — remember
attacked — march
remembered — loud
louder — attack

Part 2
Read the item and fill in the circle next to the answer.
Write the answer in the blank.

1. Jean was on night __patrol__ in this story.
   ○ planet ○ play ○ march ● patrol

2. There were __five__ moons in the night sky.
   ○ three ● five ○ third ○ six

3. The drams moved like a big __army__ when they came out of the lake.
   ● army ○ patrol ○ grasshopper ○ wake

4. The drams would __eat__ everything in their path.
   ○ stop ● eat ○ reach ○ wake

Part 3
Write the words.

grass + hopper = grasshopper
spot + light = spotlight
some + thing = something

Suffixes, comprehension items, compound words

Lesson 63

Name _____

Part 1
Write the words.

her + self = herself
what + ever = whatever
moon + light = moonlight
some + body = somebody

Part 2
Read the words in the box. Then fill in the blanks.

reached	far	shirt	closer	pressed	springs
skipped	inches	drams	pocket	melted	stabbed
eaten	barracks	messed	light	signaler	stared

Jean couldn't seem to move. She __stared__ at the drams as they came __closer__. They were only about twenty feet from her now.

"Move," she said to herself. But her legs felt as if they had __melted__.

Then Jean began to think. She __reached__ for her __signaler__. She __pressed__ the button. Lights began to flash in the __barracks__. Women began to yell, "The drams! The drams! Let's get out of here."

And Jean began to run. Now her legs felt like __springs__. Did she ever run!

Part 3
Copy the sentence.
Suddenly, a sound came from the other room.

Suddenly, a sound came from the other room.

Compound words, vocabulary/context clues, copying sentences

Lesson 64

Name _____

Part 1

The words in the first column have endings.
Write the same words without endings in the second column.

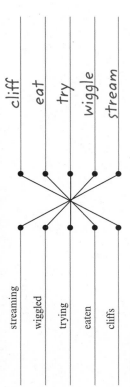

streaming	cliff
wiggled	eat
trying	try
eaten	wiggle
cliffs	stream

Part 2

Write **1, 2,** or **3** in front of each sentence to show when these things happened in the story.

___2___ Two women held Jean while the others slapped the drams.

___1___ There was a mass of drams on Jean.

___3___ Jean found out that Carla was on patrol.

Part 3

Write the name of the person each sentence tells about.

Jean   Carla   major

1. This person was not in her room. _Carla_

2. This person made a loud sound with the trumpet. _Jean_

3. This person wiggled and tried to shake off the drams. _Jean_

4. This person fell into a hole in the floor of the barracks. _Jean_

5. This person was on patrol near the cliffs. _Carla_

6. This person said, "You did a brave thing." _major_

Inflectional suffixes, sequence, characterization

Lesson 64   **113**

Lesson 65

Name _____

Part 1

Write **1, 2,** or **3** in front of each sentence to show when these things happened in the story.

___1___ Jean tried to think of everything that happened just before the drams went to sleep.

___3___ The major told the others why the trumpet made the drams sleep.

___2___ Jean gave a blast on Carla's trumpet.

Part 2

The words in the first column have endings.
Write the same words without endings in the second column.

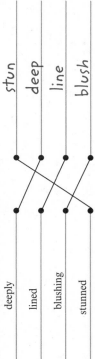

deeply	stun
lined	deep
blushing	line
stunned	blush

Part 3

Read the words in the box. Then fill in the blanks.

barracks	bubbles	blushed	sound	fill	smiled
animals	horns	hunger	felt	showed	leave
line	march	patrol	water	hungry	blast

One of the women said, "Does that mean that we can stop the drams just by blowing _horns_ when they come out of the _water_ ?"

"We can do better than that," the major said. "We can pipe _sound_ into the lake. We can keep them from getting _hungry_ for sound. Then they won't _leave_ the lake."

The women _smiled_ and looked at each other. Jean was thinking, "Now night _patrol_ won't be so bad."

Sequence, suffixes, vocabulary/context clues

Lesson 65   **115**

151